The Remnant

America's Last Days Church

Michael Scibilio

Unless otherwise stated, Scripture quotations are taken from the THE HOLY BIBLE, ENGLISH STANDARD VERSION (ESV): Scriptures taken from THE HOLY BIBLE, ENGLISH STANDARD VERSION ® Copyright© 2001 by Crossway, a publishing ministry of Good News Publishers. Used by permission.

Scripture taken from the New King James Version. Copyright © 1982 by Thomas Nelson, Inc. Used by permission.

Scripture quotations marked (NASB) are taken from the NEW AMERICAN STANDARD BIBLE® (NASB), Copyright © 1960, 1962, 1963, 1968, 1971, 1972, 1973, 1975, 1977, 1995 by The Lockman Foundation. Used by permission. www.Lockman.org.

Scripture quotations marked (NIV) are taken from the NEW INTERNATIONAL VERSION (NIV): Scripture taken from THE HOLY BIBLE, NEW INTERNATIONAL VERSION ®. Copyright© 1973, 1978, 1984, 2011 by Biblica, Inc.™. Used by permission of Zondervan

THE REMNANT

Copyright © 2020 Michael Scibilio

All rights reserved.

ISBN: 9781070936505

"Let every student be plainly instructed and earnestly pressed to consider well the end of his life and studies is to know God and Jesus Christ, which is eternal life, and therefore to lay Christ in the bottom, as the only foundation of all sound knowledge and learning."

—Harvard University 1636

THE REMNANT

CONTENTS

CHAPTER ONE

Brief Vapor – Pg. 1

Extra Dimensions – Pg. 5

Postsecularism – Pg. 15

Reality Check– Pg. 21

America's Foundation – Pg. 25

Familiarity Breeds Contempt – Pg. 32

American Jesus – Pg. 36

Mountaintop Seekers – Pg. 39

CHAPTER TWO

Church – Pg. 46

Mighty Men/New Wine – Pg. 54

The Remnant – Pg. 62

The Way – Pg. 68

Identity Crisis – Pg. 73

Influencer – Pg. 77

Revival – Pg. 83

CHAPTER THREE

Real Love – Pg. 91

Value – Pg. 94

Spirit & Truth – Pg. 97

Roadblocks – Pg. 99

The Attack on Logic – Pg. 104

Opium Drip – Pg. 107

CHAPTER FOUR

Money – Pg. 111

Anointed vs. Peddler – Pg. 114

Encounter – Pg. 118

Cover Me – Pg. 121

Not So Fast – Pg. 124

Latter Rain – Pg. 130

CHAPTER FIVE

Come Out of Her – Pg. 133

Romanism – Pg. 145

Walls Fall Supernaturally – Pg. 154

The Spirit of America – Pg. 156

Jezebel – Pg. 161

CHAPTER SIX

Ichabod – Pg. 164

Remember the Covenant – Pg. 168

Cut to the Heart – Pg. 171

Lewd Grace – Pg. 178

Vision – Pg. 181

Habitation – Pg. 184

CHAPTER SEVEN

Follow the Rainbow – Pg. 189

Signs in Sun and Moon – Pg. 196

Seek His Face – Pg. 203

Americas Final Warning – Pg. 213

The Great Falling Away – Pg. 218

THE REMNANT

My son, beware of anything beyond these. Of making many books there is no end, and much study is a weariness of the flesh. The end of the matter; all has been heard. Fear God and keep his commandments, for this is the whole duty of man. For God will bring every deed into judgment, with every secret thing, whether good or evil.[1]

---

[1] Ecclesiastes 12:12-14

CHAPTER ONE

Brief Vapor

The most peculiar thing about life is how humans mindlessly go about living it as if it's a normal thing.

Feel your heartbeat in your chest. Seriously, take a moment right now, take a deep breath, put your hand on your chest, and feel it. Every beat is another tic. Consider it your inevitable death clock. My wife told me to call it your life clock. Either way, it's going to stop sometime in the relatively near future. We all know when your heart beats its last beat your body dies within minutes. The question is, do you?

Our time here on earth is incredibly limited. The majority of people alive right now are more than halfway through their allotted earthly time limit. I'm from the state of Massachusetts but I lived in southern Florida for a little while. The state of Florida itself acts as a giant retirement community for the affluent elderly of North America. It broke my heart to walk around southern Florida and watch people with roughly ten years left to live fill their final days with golf, food, and alcohol. It was as if they were doing anything possible to avoid facing reality. The reality is, this life here on earth is exactly what God says it is, a brief vapor[2], and I don't want you to waste a single second of it!

Seriously, is anything more bizarre than life itself? Use your senses. Look around. Feel around. Analyze the surroundings that you're currently in. Be present in this moment. What is this? We're floating in space somewhere on a giant ball made up of rocks, water, and living organisms. Astronomers estimate there are more stars in the universe than grains of sand on earth. Yet here we are floating in the middle of it all complaining about the cold weather.

Life is very simple and yet amazingly complex at the same time. Take, for instance, how the realest things in life are things you can't see with your eyes, like love. You can see the effects of love in the natural, but you can't see love itself. Or how about the wind or the force we call gravity? How about those ultraviolet rays that burn your skin at the beach? We are very familiar with these invisible presences. So why is it that humans struggle with the idea of an invisible God?

Well, mankind hasn't actually struggled with this idea at all. There are many struggles you might believe mankind has that it does not because of mainstream

---

[2] **James 4:14**

projected narratives. In actuality, the idea of God is at the core of human history. The God of the Bible dates back as far as documented history goes. The Bible itself is actually the oldest, most translated, most duplicated and bestselling historical book in the history of the world. The word of God has literally shaped the world as we know it today, leaving its own unique crater in every continent around the planet.

One of the brightest men in modern history, Isaac Newton, the man who discovered calculus and the laws of the universe, was a devout Christian. It's said that he spent more time studying the Bible than he did studying science or math. He is quoted as saying, "We account the scriptures of God to be the most sublime philosophy. I find more sure marks of authenticity in the Bible than in any profane history whatsoever."[3]

The remainder of this book will be written on the basis that "All Scripture is breathed out by God and profitable for teaching, for reproof, for correction, and for training in righteousness, that the man of God may be complete, equipped for every good work"[4]. If you haven't come to that conclusion yet, please consider reading *The Case for Christ* by Lee Strobel or *Mere Christianity* by C.S. Lewis. These two books were written by once atheist men who tried to disprove Christianity and the Bible. Their

---

[3] Sir Isaac Newton Optics, 1704

[4] 2 Timothy 3:16–17

failed attempts led them both to become devout followers of Jesus. These amazing pieces of literature show you in depth, on an intellectual level, that there is no flaw in the Bible or Jesus Christ himself. Of course, you can read these books and denounce God, the Bible, and Christ Jesus, because you have the free will to think, say, and do whatever you want. People will believe whatever they choose to. That's the beauty and curse of *free will*. Reaching the point of understanding the existence of God, the inerrancy of the Bible, and the deity of Christ requires you to exercise *humility* and *faith*. Humility is a location, and it's the only place in the universe from which you can see God from. Or in the words of C.S Lewis,

"A proud man is always looking down on things and people; and, of course, as long as you are looking down, you cannot see something that is above you."[5]

---

[5] C.S. Lewis, *Mere Christianity*

Extra Dimensions

> *"...what is seen was not made out of things that are visible."* [6]

If you happen to study physics, you might be familiar with theoretical physicist Nima Arkani-Hamed. Arkani-Hamed is a professor at Princeton and has been a visiting professor at Harvard. He has many awards, degrees, and achievements attached to his name for leading the way in theoretical physics. One particular breakthrough of his really intrigues me because the Bible talks a lot about it. The following is a segment from the *Harvard Gazette*:

Arkani-Hamed's theories on extra dimensions and gravity stimulated a lot of excitement among experimental physicists, who began working to confirm his theories, said Physics Department Chair Professor Gerald Gabrielse.

> "He's particularly known for work he did that pointed out the world may have more dimensions than we're used to," Gabrielse said. "He's responsible for stimulating a lot of activity in the experimental community to confirm his theories." [7]

---

[6] Hebrews 11:3
[7] Alvin Powell, "Deconstructing dimensions to understand the universe," *Harvard Gazette*, February 6, 2003

This segment is from almost two decades ago. Since its publication it has become common practice for theoretical physicists to study and research extra dimensions. I get excited when physicists make such advancements because every step deeper they go into the layers of our universe, the more of Gods glory gets exposed for us to gaze upon. The Bible doesn't explain the physics of extra dimensions, but it does explain their logistics and reasoning.

There are greater dimensions all around us and even through us that we can't see with the naked eye. These dimensions are spiritual in nature and they take up a lot of space, much more than we might realize. Did you know that more than 99.99 percent of the human body is empty space? It's true. At the atomic level, there's mostly empty space in all visible matter and its estimated that only 5 percent of the universe is even visible to begin with. What's even more interesting is that all this "empty space" is not actually empty. There aren't any molecules or atoms present here, but there is something present that cosmologist and physicists have been noticing and it's all around the universe. They call it "dark matter." This terminology is rather misleading because the matter isn't "dark" it's transparent or unseen. This transparent matter has loads of energy and modern science is just now starting to scratch the surface of what it actually is.

When trying to understand extra dimensions we must first reflect on the three dimensions most people are familiar with. These are easily understood in length, width and height that make up depth. We humans are currently bound to three-dimensional bodies in a three-dimensional world that rotates in the fourth-dimension, *time*.

Hypothetically speaking, if there was someone living on the surface of a perfectly flat piece of paper in two dimensions, they wouldn't be able to fully comprehend an object from a greater dimension if they encountered it. For example, if something from the third dimension, like a snowball, started approaching the person living in the two-dimensional paper world, they would only be able to perceive the incoming snowball as a flat, growing white circle. They would never be able to perceive or understand the entirety or complexity of the snowball while living in a two-dimensional world. The same goes for us humans in a three-dimensional world when trying to perceive something from a greater dimension.

The rather famous physicist, Michio Kaku, likes to explain extra dimensions by standing over a theoretical two-dimensional fishpond. If we were looking down at the fish with eyes on the sides of their heads, we could watch them go left, right, back and forward. We in the third dimension would be invisible to them. For we live in a world of *"up"* that is incomprehensible to them. In their world it would be presumed as foolishness to imagine another world outside or above their linear world. Referring to this fishpond concept, Dr. Kaku said, "what happens if I reach down and grab one of the fish, lift the fish up. Maybe that fish was a scientist and the scientist would say, "bah humbug, science fiction, there's no world of *up, up* does not exist!" Well I would grab this scientist, lift them up in the world of *up*, hyperspace the third dimension. What would he see? He would see beings breathing without water…a new law of biology… beings moving without fins… a new law of physics, and then I would put the fish back into the pond, what kind of stories would he tell? Well today we physicists believe, we cannot prove it yet, but we are the fish"[8].

I love this analogy because it's incredibly biblical. We humans are indeed the fish! There have even been fish like the apostle Paul that have been pulled up into the world of *"up."* Just like in Dr. Kakus analogy! When Paul was pulled "up" he wasn't sure if he was even in his own body or not. Being "caught up" in the Bible is the word *harpazo* in Greek, which is also used for *rapture* in English. *(More on this later)*.

I don't know the exact number of dimensions that exist or how they function paired with our known dimensions. What I do know is that they are invisible or "behind the veil" of what is visible. Many physicists believe these extra dimensions are warped right around our

---

[8] Michio Kaku Jan 29, 2016
2016https://www.youtube.com/watch?time_continue=3&v=RUlVFzl_BJs&feature=emb_title

current vision. Behind this veil, God has given us distinct insight into three separate layers of heaven, two ancient realms in the depths of the earth and a kingdom of the air all around us. Within these invisible dimensions there are many living beings that are not human. There are also many humans there that are no longer bound to their material body. There is much more going on in the universe than meets the eye. Whether you believe in God or not, the vast majority of what goes on in the universe is simply invisible to the naked eye.

Gods intellect is lightyears beyond ours. God calls trillions of stars in the universe by their own individual name.[9] If God calls the stars by their own name, I'm sure they have a bigger purpose than just decoration. Theoretical physics, even through a biblical lens, can leave you pondering some very heavy, deep thoughts about the functionality of life and the universe.

It's important that we don't get too sidetracked by the complexities of the universe because there's far more important things at hand in this brief vapor than discovery. That is why Isaac Newton studied the word of God more than science or math. What God has made known to us *now* is far more important than the unknowns of life and the universe. What God has made known to us now is the *purpose of life*, and the *why* is much more important than the *how*.

---

[9] Psalm 147:4

This will change your life forever if you receive this; *Jesus Christ* is the key to understanding life itself. The time Jesus spent in our three-dimensional fishpond forever shook the world because his life defied time, physics, biology and even death.

The purpose of your life is a person. His name is Jesus.

"I pray that the eyes of your heart may be enlightened in order that you may know the hope to which he has called you, the riches of his glorious inheritance in his holy people, and his incomparably great power for us who believe. That power is the same as the mighty strength he exerted when he raised Christ from the dead and seated him at his right hand in the heavenly realms, far above all rule and authority, power and dominion, and every name that is invoked, not only in the present age but also in the one to come. And God placed all things under his feet and appointed him to be head over everything for the church, which is his body, the fullness of him who fills everything in every way."[10]

All of these dimensions around us are a footstool for Jesus! He rests his feet on our fishpond and comes into it at will.

---

[10] Ephesian 1:18-23

The Son made physical appearances all throughout ancient history. They're often referred to as *Christophanies*. Jesus of Nazareth is God himself coming into his creation in the likeness of his creation. Let that sink in for a minute. Jesus is just as much man as he is God. Why did God come to earth in the form of a man? Why did the Creator take on the form of his creation? The answer is found in one word, *love*.

"I pray that you, being rooted and established in love, may have power, together with all the Lord's holy people, to grasp **how wide and long and high and deep** is the **love** of Christ, and to know this *love* that surpasses knowledge—that you may be filled to the measure of all the fullness of God."[11]

Wide, long, high, deep, sound familiar? The love of Jesus fills our dimensions! Jesus himself *is* love[12] and he fills all things! Jesus is the fullness of all things! The purpose of life is *love*; his name is Jesus! If this concept doesn't fully register in your mind, good! Because his love *surpasses knowledge*! It's meant to humble you! God became man and stayed man because it was *Loves* greatest way to become intimate with his most loved creation, *YOU!*

---

[11] Ephesians 3:17-19
[12] 1 John 4:7

Physicists and cosmologist acknowledge an attribute within "dark matter" that literally holds all things in the universe together in place. They recognize that without it the stars of the universe would be flung away at astronomical speeds. What most physicists and cosmologists don't realize that they're picking up on is actually *Jesus himself.* Yes, Jesus!

"And he (*Jesus*) is before all things, and in him **all things hold together.**"[13]

Jesus not only fills all things; in him all things are held together! The man who wrote this information 2000 years ago (Paul) was pulled up into the world of *"up"* and witnessed the *omnipresence* of Christ in a way we cannot! Christ Jesus himself is a dynamic mystery that was revealed to mankind 2000 years ago!

Jesus is the most famous man in the history of the earth for a reason. He is God, He is the Word and He is Love. In Him are hidden all the treasures of wisdom and knowledge.

"...to reach all the riches of full assurance of understanding

---

[13] Colossians 1:17

> and the knowledge of God's mystery, which is Christ, in whom are hidden all the treasures of wisdom and knowledge."[14]

These revelations of reality are hidden treasures of wisdom and knowledge within Christ himself. That is why Christ desires to put his Spirit within you. He wants you to receive the fullness of life, which is himself. This is another one of the great mysteries of life that has been revealed to us through Gods word. God desires to put *HIS SPIRIT* in *YOU*!

> "the mystery that has been kept hidden for ages and generations, but is now disclosed to the Lord's people. To them God has chosen to make known among the Gentiles the glorious riches of this mystery, which is Christ in you, the hope of glory."[15]

    There are many stories in the Bible that show us a glimpse of what's going on around us in these unseen extra dimensions. Many of these stories are filled with angelic and demonic beings that seem to defy the laws of physics. Jesus himself was able to walk on water because he wasn't

---

[14] Colossians 2:2-3
[15] Colossians 1:26-27

bound by our dimensions or by our laws of physics.

Colossians 1:16 says, "For by him all things were created, in heaven and on earth, visible and invisible, whether thrones or dominions or rulers or authorities—all things were created through him and for him."

Visible and invisible, all things were made by Jesus and for Jesus. Jesus isn't bound by anything including gravity or the fourth known dimension we cling so tightly to, *time*.

Biblical prophecy is simply God speaking into the fabric of the fourth dimension (time) from where he dwells, outside of time (a greater dimension). God speaks through mankind by his Holy Spirit. That's why dozens of detailed writings exist today about the life of Jesus that were written hundreds of years before he was born. God knows the beginning from the end. Jesus was prophesied about hundreds of years before he was born. His birthplace was even prophesied roughly 700 years before he was born. The prophet Daniel gave us the exact day that Jesus would be born hundreds of years prior to his birth. *You don't have to have faith to believe this.* You can view the ancient manuscripts yourself. How do you think those "wise men" made it all the way to find Jesus as a child? The Magi came from far east where Daniel was held in Babylonian captivity. The Magi, who were actually some of the most educated men alive in that time period, would have studied Daniel's prophecies predicting the birth of the King. They also studied astrology, which is used often by God to show *signs of the times (more on this later)*.

This life here on earth is just the very beginning. Do not waste it on three dimensional things! The natural man only thinks about his next fifty years. The supernatural man or women, infused with the Spirit of God, thinks eternally, they think through the Spirit of God, they think in a greater dimension, they think *outside of time*. That is why the true remnant of Gods people can trade in everything this world has to offer, just to know Jesus.

"Indeed, I count everything as loss because of the surpassing worth of knowing Christ Jesus my Lord. For his sake I have suffered the loss of all things and count them as rubbish, in order that I may gain Christ" Philippians 3:8

I implore you to get to know Jesus today, he's much closer than you might realize. Just call upon his name.

Postsecularism

The argument for intelligent design is seeing a resurgence among the intellectual elites who once discredited the idea of there being a *Creator*. The recent advancements in microbiology that were simply unavailable to Darwin are shattering his theory of cross-species evolution into pieces. The possibility of one species turning into another is limited to the point of impossibility by time itself and the immensely different variations and likelihood of failed mutations at the cellular level. Recently, during a sit-down interview between Yale professor Dr. David Gelernter and New York Times bestselling author Dr. Stephen Meyer of the Discovery Institute (two men who currently denounce Darwin's theory of evolution), the topic of creation came up, and it sparked an interesting train of thought from Dr. Stephen Meyer:

> What we know from experience is information whether we find it in a hieroglyphic inscription or a paragraph in a book or information embedded in a radio signal or in a section of computer code wherever we find information and we trace it back to its ultimate source we always come to a mind not a material process…These undirected evolutionary mechanisms that have been proposed as an explanation of the origin of information fail for various reasons.[1]

In other words, you wouldn't see an explosion in a junkyard result in something as intricately designed and polished as a Ferrari. While it is understood by biologist that a single human cell is more intricate and polished than

---

[1] David Berlinski, "Mathematical Challenges To Darwin's Theory Of Evolution, With David Berlinski, Stephen Meyer, And David Gelernter," *Hoover Institution*, July 22, 2019, https://www.hoover.org/research/mathematical-challenges-darwins-theory-evolution-david-berlinski-stephen-meyer-and-david.

an entire metropolitan city, never mind a car, somehow for several generations secular science got stuck on this idea that life appeared from virtually nothing.

With many of the world's leading minds starting to head in the same direction as Dr. Meyer and Dr. Gelernter, it is only a matter of time before Darwinism as we know it is lain to rest as a theory of old. It may take a few generations for it to fade away—the many educators who have dedicated their lives to the religion of Darwinism will not give up easily—but I'm thoroughly convinced Darwinism will not be known for what it is today in the fairly near future.

In 2004 Paleontologist Mary Schweitzer discovered a Tyrannosaurs rex skeleton buried in a Montana canyon.[16] Dr. Schweitzer cut open a large bone from the T-Rex and what she discovered changed the science world forever. *Well... it should have.* Unfortunately, there's a good chance you've never even heard of Mary Schweitzer. What was by far the greatest discovery in modern paleontology was quickly buried back up by other scientists.

Inside the supposed *"65 million"* year old T-Rex thigh bone, Dr. Schweitzer found pliable tissue that was reddish brown in color. The substance was further analyzed and proven to contain red blood cells. This caused quite the uproar in the science world. However, it was quickly

---

[16] Dr. Mary Schweitzer discovers T-rex blood cells Horizon Dinosaurs: The Hunt for Life, BBC Two

covered up by farfetched evolutionist theories. The humble Dr. Schweitzer was bullied right out of the science worlds inner spotlight. Red blood cells couldn't even come close to surviving one million years in the ground, never mind sixty-five million.

The truth is, dinosaurs walked the earth roughly 6,000 years ago, but no matter how many dead whales we find in the Andes mountains[17], many secular scientists would simply rather die than admit that their life's studies were built on theories of evolution that aren't accurate. The truth is, God destroyed the earth with water and he's going to destroy it again very soon with fire[18].

Physical adaptations have been occurring since the beginning of documented history. We have seen mountain-dwelling people groups develop barrel chests over generations to breathe in more oxygen, beaks grow longer to allow certain birds to reach their food inside trees, and human skin color darkens in locations with greater UV ray exposure. All of these adaptations are examples of intelligent design.

When God made animals, he made them according to their *kind*: "And God made the beasts of the earth according to their kinds and the livestock according to their kinds, and everything that creeps on the ground according to its kind. And God saw that it was good" (Genesis 1:25).

---

[17] *This isn't an exaggeration. Fish fossils are found on mountains all over the world. Whales were literally found in the Andes.*
[18] Isaiah 66:15

Herein lies the key to unlocking the individual species-specific genetic code. The ancient Hebrew word that was used for *kinds* in this passage is מִין (*min*), which literally means "species." When God made mankind, he made him in his image and his likeness. That is why we are so incredibly different than any other living creature on earth. You were made in the image and likeness of God! Humans and animals are both intelligently designed, but humans are set apart with a spirit in the likeness of God, for God is spirit (John 4:24). God put in us a spirit that connected us to his spiritual gene pool. It pleased God to make family (us) in his likeness so we could have an intimate relationship with him unlike any other being in the history of the universe.

All of God's creation is subject to a range of adaptations according to their kind or (species). I surely can't eat the same meal as someone who grew up in rural India and not get sick. I simply never developed the same enzymes they did. Physical and mental adaptations are passed down genetically through generations. Adaptations themselves have limits at the molecular level. Adaptations only come from the code that **already exists** inside the humans' or animals' DNA. These adaptations always *benefit* the individual human or animal. The theory of cross-species evolution is NOT related to adaptation. The theory of evolution relies on "successful mutations" of DNA, which rarely, if ever, happen. Depending on what one might consider "successful" in the first place. Generally, anything mutated from its original condition ends up in a **much worse** condition than its original state. A clear example of this is the 120,000 babies that are born in America every year that have harmful mutations. These birth *defects* are known as things like Down syndrome, blindness, deafness, club foot, spina bifida, cleft lip, and congenital heart disease. Although certain knowledge is increasing, the earth and its inhabitants are not advancing but decaying under the repercussions of sin (Isaiah 24:5–6).

    Postsecularism in the context I'm using the word is simply a resurgence of religious and spiritual beliefs. Modern secularism is fading away and mankind is becoming more spiritually "primitive". I believe this postsecular movement will be the final wave of "enlightenment" to bring unity and peace to this decaying world. The spiritual and more important reason why the world is headed in a unified postsecular direction is because the world as we know it is coming to an end. Jesus Christ is coming back for his remnant people very soon.

    Over the last seventy years, every continent in the world has gone through unprecedented Christian revival. North America is currently in the back of the "revival pack." However, recently around the world hundreds of millions of people have come to put their faith in the one true God, Christ Jesus. But here is the catch. The Antichrist is coming into power soon, and his spirit is rising. He will claim to be the one God above all gods *(2 Thessalonians 2:4)*. Satan himself is in support of the world going back to a "creator mindset" so he himself can claim to be the creator. He will do so, and he will deceive the world with a form of unified spirituality. The Antichrist will bring unity to multiple religions in the Middle East.

Creationism is on the rise, but so is deception. Lord willing, by the end of this book you will be equipped enough to discern the truth from the ever-increasing deception of the enemy and his kingdom of the air all around us.

Reality Check

When we come to put our faith in Jesus, we have to relearn everything we thought we knew about life through the filter of God's word. We must become like newborn children with unlearned minds. This may seem extreme to some, but this is an absolutely necessary first step. This is the essence of being *"born again"*. Baptizing and renewing the mind through the washing of God's word is the only way to avoid bringing any worldly wisdom into your new life and the body of Christ.

The Bible talks about two separate categories of wisdom, earthly wisdom and heavenly wisdom:

"But if you have bitter jealousy and selfish ambition in your hearts, do not boast and be false to the truth. This is not the wisdom that comes down from above, but is earthly, unspiritual, demonic....But the wisdom from above is first

> pure, then peaceable, gentle, open to reason, full of mercy and good fruits, impartial and sincere."[19]

All earthly wisdom is demonic in nature. It comes from the father of lies himself. The goal of earthly wisdom is to exalt oneself over everyone else, and its main driving force is pride. Earthly wisdom can certainly be effective. It can help bring you greater prosperity and glory. But the reality of your existence is that you were created to bring glory to God, not yourself. That is why it is essential to relearn the reality of your existence through the word of God.

The Bible tells us that the fear of the Lord is the beginning of knowledge (Proverbs 1:7). Therefore, unless you fear God you really can't comprehend reality itself, never mind its complexities. Fifty thousand people a year in America make the horrific decision to end their own life. I believe this is partially the fault of our standard education system in America. Our current science curriculum indoctrinates over 50 million students every year by teaching them that they are an animal and their great ancestor is a squid. When you're taught at a young age that life is meaningless and you have no worth, it changes the mental pocket of reality you live in.

Reality is not subjective. What I mean by that is there are zero variables in the reality of our existence. You cannot actually change or alter reality. However, we were

---

[19] James 3:14,17

made in the image of the Creator and carry his likeness. Since we have creator DNA mixed with sin, we have the tendency to create our own mental pockets of reality to live in. With all the confusion in the world, reality has become a choice. The reality we choose to live in takes place in the mind. That is why the enemy (Satan) is always attacking the mind, and why mental illness in America is at an all-time high. The mind is the battlefield in the war for our souls, the middle ground between the spirit realm and the natural realm. Your mind is interdimensional space. This is why it is so important for us to take every thought captive (2 Corinthians 10:5).

In America, our society is geared toward and set on mission to accomplish things that have no eternal value. Millions of people live in the virtual realities of video games, social media, and TV. Others spend their entire lives trying to mass enormous amounts of money just to die and take none of it with them. The average man can't see how worthless these realities are because the average man has no fear of the Lord and therefore no foundation of knowledge to build upon.[20] The truth is that anything in this life that is not done for the glory of God has *zero* eternal value or purpose.

God's word says, "Where your treasure is, there your heart will be also" (Matthew 6:21). If your heart is with Jesus, your rewards are in heaven with him. It doesn't matter what your bank account looks like. As long as

---

[20] Authors paraphrase of Proverbs 1:7

you're living in the will of God, you'll find true contentment. The only way to be in the will of God, however, is to first choose to live in his reality which is the one true reality.

The Bible is your how-to manual for living in the reality God created. It's only through reading God's word that we can understand the depths of real life and what is truly important. Just admitting that the Bible is really Gods word is not enough either. Acknowledging his word to be true is not the same as saving faith. You can know the truth without making it your truth. You have free will. You can stay living in your own self-made reality with your own self-made moral code, but you'll always be living a lie.

I know many people who profess the word of God to be true yet continue to live in a way that, according to that very same word of God, leads to hell. It's hard to process this obvious negligence of truth. There seems to be this part of the brain that pushes off uncomfortable thoughts that the flesh doesn't want to hear and then creates its own bubble of reality to live in instead. That's really the best way to explain it. There are men who know they have cancer and continue to live in denial of it. It doesn't mean they don't have cancer. People create their own realities and then live in them because humans are disobedient by nature and are often afraid to face the discomfort of real life.

The reason I'm writing this book is because I love you and I don't want you to miss out on what is truly important in life. My hope is that this book will open your eyes to any false reality you might be living in. I don't want to just present you with the truth. I deeply desire for you to know the *TRUTH* personally. His name is Jesus and he said, "I am the way, and the *TRUTH*, and the life. No one comes to the Father except through me" (John 14:6).

America's Foundation

Since the beginning of time God has continuously preserved a remnant of his people that will worship him in spirit and in truth. Four hundred years ago, a remnant of God's people was extracted from Europe and deposited in the New World we call America. It's important we start endeavoring into the reality of our existence with the story of our forefathers, for they built the foundation of this nation and its their prayers that we stand on today.

Every building has a foundation. The foundation is the largest contributor to the building's structural integrity. If you try to construct a building without first laying a concrete foundation, that structure simply will not stay standing. This is the concept Jesus taught about in the book of Matthew. He said, you're foolish if you try to build a structure on anything but solid rock. The rain will come down, the streams will rise, and the wind will blow, reducing it to rubble.[21] We know he was speaking metaphorically. He was speaking about our lives, their structure and his vital role in them, but this wisdom goes even deeper. It can likewise be applied to societal structure.

If there is no concrete, rock-solid moral base for a society to stand on, it will collapse. What is morally right for one person could be morally wrong for another person. This kind of opinionated division is like the wind and the rain Jesus talked about. Mankind is double minded in all he does. His opinions and feelings will erode an entire society unless there is a foundation that doesn't move. This is exactly what we see happening in America today. Before analyzing the current condition of our nation, I want to look deeper into its foundation. The foundation that has made America the most prosperous world-leading nation in modern history.

October 31, 1517. The Roman Catholic Church was selling "get-out-of-hell-free cards" known as indulgences. You could even buy one of these "tickets to heaven" for a dead family member. A theology professor by the name of Martin Luther would boldly address the Catholic Church about this non-biblical act of greed and simultaneously expose dozens of other heretic Catholic practices. He wrote a letter containing ninety-five corrections to the Catholic Church's false doctrine and nailed it to the door of *All Saints Church* in Wittenberg, Germany. This became known as Martin Luther's Ninety-five Theses. Luther sent

---

[21] Authors paraphrasing of Mathew 7:24-25

a copy of his theses to every church in greater Germany. This was the spark that started the Protestant Reformation.

The Protestant Reformation spread like wildfire across Europe. European citizens started to take notice of the unbiblical doctrine the Roman Catholic Church was teaching. They felt taken advantage of and demanded change. Many people of that time period could not read, and the ones who could were not able to read the Bible because it was not translated into many languages yet.

In 1534, England broke ties with the Roman Catholic Church. Protestant reformers, later known as Puritans for their attempt to "purify" themselves from the Catholic Church, joined the reformed Church of England. A smaller group within the Puritan movement still saw unbiblical practice in the Church of England and the puritan movement itself. It was all still too "Catholic" for them. That smaller group became known as Separatists. These Separatists were inspired by the Word of God to break away completely (separate) from the Church of England. They were driven to start a society of their own that would actually live according to God's word. Their hearts were set to restore the church to the original state of the New Testament followers of Jesus.

It all started with a "house church" in the home of an English official named William Brewster. The congregation would gather there often to pray, take communion, read the Bible and have fellowship with one another. Eventually they organized themselves into a

Congregational Church in 1606. Future governor William Bradford joined this small home church despite the mockery of his neighbors and the rejection of his own extended family. William Bradford was a respected scholar, an intellectual who spoke five languages. This was not the popular style of "church" for him to be seen in. The Separatists denounced the Anglican Prayer book and Queen Elizabeth's episcopacy (mans imposed religion). The Church of England was offended and felt threatened by this movement, so they heavily persecuted the Separatists congregation. The only option the Separatists had left was to flee England all together.

John Robinson, the Separatists pastor, studied at the University of Cambridge a few years after William Brewster had studied there himself. Jon Robinson was one of the first to encourage the idea of separation of church and state. This idea was biblical, and it would give power to the body of Christ, the congregation, the remnant. Pastor Robinson taught the Separatists to think for themselves and read the word of God freely. Through doing so his congregation developed their own personal relationships with the living God and left behind the dead religion of their forefathers.

After facing many obstacles, relocations and hardships, the remnant of 1620 (known today as the Pilgrims) set sail west from Holland on a ship called the Mayflower. The Mayflower is very relatable to Noah's Ark. God was preserving a people who would worship him in spirit and in truth, a people who genuinely loved him, a people who would seek to preserve Gods kingdom and not their own lives, a people who would strive for obedience and right standing with God, a people whom God would use to light the world with the truth.

The Pilgrims left Holland due to the corrupt society there that was influencing their own children. For the glory of God and the advancement of the Christian faith they decided to head to the newly "found" Virginia Colony to seek freedom, refuge and opportunity. After sixty-six days at sea, having been thrown off course by violent weather, the Mayflower anchored on the tip of modern-day Cape Cod. They searched for habitable land for weeks but were detoured by hostile Natives. Finally, mid-December 1620 the Pilgrims dropped their anchor in modern-day Plymouth, Massachusetts. Shortly after their arrival in Plymouth, Jamestown, Virginia fell apart at the seams. Jamestown was plagued with disease, malnutrition, and poor relations with the Powhatan Natives. It's crucial that people understand Jamestown was an extension of the same Church of England that the Separatists of Plymouth Colony were fleeing. I'm not saying there weren't any true believers in Virginia, but the Jamestown settlers heavily imposed their religion on all who endeavored into their society. God providentially shifted the winds of the Atlantic for the Separatists to land far away from any Virginia settlement.

The settlement of Plymouth faced initial hardships to say the least. Half of their 102 passengers died that first winter. However, by the grace of God, and the prayers of the remnant, they were able to rebound from that tragic winter. The Pilgrims were blessed with amazing natural resources. The land of Plymouth Colony itself was simply unappealing to the local Wampanoag tribe because disease had previously killed a large population in the area and therefore, the Wampanoags considered it cursed land. Governor William Bradford met with the local chief, Massasoit, and developed a peace treaty with the Wampanoags. The Plymouth Colony would purchase any extended land from Chief Massasoit. The Natives and the Pilgrims would regularly meet in fellowship thanks to the miraculous godsend of Squanto, the local native who was learning the English language right across the English Channel from the Pilgrims years before their arrival in Plymouth.

Bradford once stated, "Nevertheless, to keep a good conscience, and walk in such a way as God has prescribed in his word, is a thing which I must prefer before you all, and above life itself." This statement speaks so clearly of the hearts of the Pilgrims. Above all other ambitions they so desired to lead lives that honored God according to his word, and so the Pilgrims risked their lives to establish a society that would not manipulate the word of God but lay it as its moral foundation and basis of all understanding. (It should be noted that not all 102 passengers on the Mayflower were God fearing men and women. Some were only traveling to make money in the New World.)

On November 11th, 1620 the pilgrim men drafted the Mayflower Compact, which was the first governing document of the United States, and it was indeed structured upon biblical principles. This covenant was formed in the sight of God and man and it marked our nation forever.

Plymouth became a prosperous settlement, attracting many new settlers from Europe. Plymouth, Massachusetts is the longest continually occupied colony in America, and it is still expanding today. Thousands of other Protestants fleeing persecution in England shortly followed the path of these faithful pioneers.

Fast forward ~~156~~ 163 years. The year is ~~1776~~ 1783, the Revolutionary War is over. The United States was victorious. England no longer had any say in what happened in the New World. The Declaration of Independence was drafted and signed by the nation's elect leaders, twenty-seven of whom had Christian seminary degrees from institutions such as Harvard and Yale. Yes, you read that correctly; Harvard and Yale were originally Christian institutions. Harvard's original mission statement once stated:

"Let every student be plainly instructed and earnestly pressed to consider well the end of his life and studies is to know God and Jesus Christ, which is eternal life, and therefore to lay Christ in the bottom, as the only foundation of all sound knowledge and learning."

In fact, biblical teaching was at the core of standard

education in the United States public school system all the way up until 1962 when the Supreme Court banned mandatory Bible reading in public schools, even though just a few years prior in 1956 President Eisenhower had decreed "In God We Trust" must appear on American currency. There is no mistaking that the God on our currency is the God of the Bible, and there is no mistaking the close relationship between the United States of America and the word of God. The Bible has always been our moral foundation and source of truth.

To this day, roughly 70 percent of the United States still claims they belong to the Christian faith. There is a church on every road from Maine to California. We sing "God Bless America" at sporting events and tattoo crosses on our bodies. As a nation we start celebrating Jesus's birthday months in advance, whether it's for him or not. Many people sat through church as children hearing in-depth stories about the life of Jesus. I would even imagine there isn't a single American citizen who has not heard about Jesus. *And I believe this has become the problem.*

Familiarity Breeds Contempt

There are two major hurdles in getting to know someone personally. The first is preconception, and the second is intimacy. In this subchapter we are going to address the first obstacle, preconception.

In roughly 30AD, Jesus started his ministry throughout Israel. At the beginning of his ministry he performed miracle upon miracle. The apostle John said he did so many miraculous things that if every one of them was written down the world itself could not contain the number of books it would amount to.

Jesus constantly drew a massive crowd of people wherever he went during his years of ministry. Sometimes these crowds reached 20,000 plus. People were drawn to him because word was quickly spreading about his amazing *godlike* abilities and teachings. It seemed as if everything was going smoothly, until he and his disciples arrived in Nazareth, Jesus's hometown. Now, you might naturally think that Jesus's hometown[22] would be full of his biggest fans, but it was actually quite the opposite. He arrived in Nazareth and taught as rabbis did on the Sabbath. Instead of rightly marveling at his wisdom, the people of Nazareth said, "Is this not the carpenter, the son of Mary and brother of James and Joses and Judas and Simon? And aren't his sisters here with us?" (Mark 6:3) They were offended by him.

The people of Nazareth were familiar with Jesus, but their faulty preconception of him bred contempt in their hearts. Contempt is the feeling that a thing or a person is beneath consideration, worthless, or deserving of scorn. Wherever contempt for Jesus is, the Spirit of the living God

---

[22] Archeologist suggest that Nazareth was a small town with less than 200 people in it at the time of Jesus.

is not welcome.

"Familiarity breeds contempt" has been a common saying throughout history, but one of its first known introductions came in a fable by Aesop in 620–560 BC:

When first the Fox saw the Lion he was terribly frightened, and ran away and hid himself in the wood. Next time however he came near the King of Beasts he stopped at a safe distance and watched him pass by. The third time they came near one another the Fox went straight up to the Lion and passed the time of day with him, asking him how his family were, and when he should have the pleasure of seeing him again; then turning his tail, he parted from the Lion without much ceremony.

"Familiarity Breeds Contempt"[1]

The reader knows that the Fox really knew nothing about the Lion and that the King of Beasts could have stepped on the little Fox at any moment and squashed him. The Fox became familiar with the Lion, and the preconception he developed was far from an accurate assessment. How many

---

[1] Æsop, "Fables, retold by Joseph Jacobs," *The Harvard Classics*, ed. Charles W. Eliot, vol. 17 (New York: P.F. Collier & Son, 1909–14; Bartleby.com, 2001), www.bartleby.com/17/1/.

of us have turned our tail in arrogance toward God?

The people of Nazareth had grown up with Jesus. He was just an average "Joe carpenter" in their eyes. His brothers and sisters were known throughout the town and probably had their own loads of dirty laundry that people knew about. Jesus the humble carpenter was not who they expected to be at the center of a massive crowd, never mind the Messiah, fulfilling hundreds of years of Biblical prophecy. They were all too familiar with Jesus the local boy to see who was really in their midst: God incarnate.

Preconception has misled me a lot in my life. I try really hard to let people show me who they are before thinking I have them figured out. We must do the same with Jesus; preconception hinders intimacy. As long as we continue to have preconceived ideas about who Jesus is, we will never get to know him personally. You can't live through someone else's relationship with Jesus, and you can't truly know Jesus unless you can get past all the preconceived ideas you have about him.

God directly opposes pride, and pride is the heart of contempt. The contempt for Jesus in Nazareth disabled the power of God from moving in their city because they put themselves in direct opposition of God.[23] Stale familiarity with a false, dead Jesus has developed contempt in the heart of the average American toward the real, living Jesus and his Spirit. I believe the current contempt for Jesus in

---

[23] ... "God opposes the proud but gives grace to the humble." James 4:6

America, especially within the church, is hindering the outpouring of his Spirit across the land.

American Jesus

The problem with everyone in America "knowing" Jesus is that the vast majority of people who claim to know him don't actually know him. As we saw in Mark chapter six, no one really knew Jesus in his own hometown. America has become the new hometown of Jesus. Most families were brought up around him and have a preconceived idea about who he is. The United States was established on the foundation of Jesus and his word. Christianity itself is intertwined into the fabric of our society whether we choose to admit it or not.

Over the last 400 years there have been far more false Christians than actual Christians in the United States. What I mean by this is most self-proclaimed Christians in America don't actually live to the biblical qualification or standard of the term *Christian*.

I can tell everyone that I'm an astronaut. I can wear NASA gear and even talk to people about celestial coordinates and my future mission to Mars. But the reality is, I'm not an astronaut, even if I truly believe that I am. This is the same with being a follower of Jesus. I can pretend all I want that I'm a Christian. I can even fool myself into thinking I am. But if my life isn't truly subject to the authority of Christ, I am not a follower of Jesus. Period. So many people throughout our nation wear the title of Christ follower and yet Christ doesn't have any say over their lives. In fact, a majority of these "Christians" live lives that are completely contradictory to what Jesus taught.

I've heard it said that 93 percent of Christians will never share their faith in Jesus. Jesus said himself, "For whoever is ashamed of me and of my words, of him will the Son of Man be ashamed when he comes in his glory and the glory of the Father and of the holy angels" (Luke 9:26). Therefore, the real question we need to ask ourselves is, out of that 93 percent, how many are truly Christians in the eyes of God?

Faulty Christian behavior has led the average person outside the church to not want anything to do with Jesus, the Bible, or Christianity, and I don't blame them. The biggest problem with the Christian faith has continued to be the self-proclaimed "Christian" themselves who live in sin. In my lifetime alone, I've witnessed literally thousands of Catholic priests become exposed as child molesters, which has directly affected millions of Americans' lives. Who wants a Jesus who is associated with that? I sure don't! These "Christians" are just as bad as the "Christians" who parade around shouting hate speech at people living in homosexuality. Last time I checked Jesus died for their sin too!

But the most deceptive and possibly most

destructive "Christian" is the one who attends church every week for many years and possibly even serves in the church or holds a position in ministry but continues to live a life that is conformed to the world. The Bible is crystal clear: "Do not be conformed to this world, but be transformed by the renewal of your mind, that by testing you may discern what is the will of God, what is good and acceptable and perfect"[24]

There needs to be a higher standard for labeling oneself a follower of Christ—the same standard that God gave us in his word. The Christian is not supposed to look like the world, act like the world, desire the things of the world, do what the world does, listen to what the world listens to, watch what the world watches, speak like the world speaks, or think like the world thinks.

This doesn't mean we are supposed to try and obtain some high level of righteousness in our own strength. We could never make ourselves holy enough for God through our own works. It's only by God's grace we are saved through faith in him. It's only by the blood of Jesus that we are made righteous and its only by spending time with him we pick up his desires and lose ours. You become like those you spend time with. If you become madly in love with Jesus, you'll start to reflect his image. When you have true fellowship with the Holy Spirit, he'll start to reveal things in your life that don't belong and have to change. This is called sanctification. Sanctification is a

---

[24] Romans 12:2

lifelong process of God conforming you into his image for his good work and good pleasure. He does this so you'll be more effective for the kingdom of God. He does this so you'll have less in your life hindering your own relationship with him. He does this so your life will show a truer reflection of him and his character to the world. God wants his ambassadors to represent him properly on earth. Christianity without a true relationship with the living God is dead religion. God desires your heart, not your religion. This leads us to the second hurdle in getting to know someone: Intimacy.

Mountaintop Seekers

Being intimate with someone suggests a close familiarity between you and that person. This only develops by spending countless hours together. Think about the closest, most intimate relationship you have with another individual human. Well, Jesus desires an even closer and more intimate relationship with you. However, that only comes by spending vulnerable time with him, letting him search your heart and renew your mind through the washing of his word. There is no greater place than the secret place with Jesus, and no place the enemy is trying harder to keep you from. It's in the secret place when no one is watching that you develop true intimacy with God. You will only want Jesus to the measure that you see him. This is why the greatest of all spiritual warfare is aimed specifically at breaking your eye contact with Jesus. You can't want him unless you see him! You can't know him unless look into his eyes.

When you are adopted into sonship in Christ, the enemy's tactics don't change. He still does everything he can to keep you from Jesus. He'll even use "good things" to keep you from spending time with Jesus. He'll tell you to listen to a podcast or just watch half of an uplifting sermon online before going to bed. He'll do anything to keep you from actually meeting with Jesus in the secret place, because he knows that the secret place is where we gather our strength and power.

"He who dwells in the secret place of the Most High Shall abide under the shadow of the Almighty."
Psalms 91:1 (NKJV)

There are two mountaintop seekers I want to introduce to you that you are probably familiar with: Moses and Elijah. They lived about 300 years apart, but interestingly enough, they were united with Jesus in the book of Matthew on the mount of transfiguration. Moses died a natural human death and Elijah was supernaturally taken up to heaven by God roughly 1000 years or so before meeting with Jesus on the mount of transfiguration. Matthew writes of the close intimate relationship between Jesus, Moses and Elijah as they gathered. The disciples Peter, James and John were simply blessed to have been there to witness this sight of Jesus in his natural state of glory. The amazing thing about this gathering on the mountaintop was the fact that Jesus was meeting two men that he met with separately at different times, hundreds of years prior on the top of Mount Sinai. It's through their lives we can learn about the second hurdle of getting to know someone, intimacy.

Moses is our first mountaintop seeker. Moses was considered the most humble man on the face of the earth. During the time he was alive he was also the closest in relation to God on earth. There is a direct correlation between our humility and our closeness to God.

Moses was special, you could say. No one else was able to climb Mount Sinai at that time and talk to God. Actually, if they tried, they'd be killed for touching just the base of the mountain. The cloud that covered Mount Sinai acted as a veil to cover Gods glory, similar to the veil that covered up the Holy of Holies in the tabernacle. What an incredible honor it was for one man, Moses, to be able to ascend upon the mountain, walk through the veil and into the presence of Almighty God.

When Jesus died on the cross for your sins, the physical and spiritual temple veil was torn from top to bottom, allowing *you* to ascend into the Holy of Holies, into the presence of God. Yes, you, blood-bought believer. The atonement has been made for your transgressions. The blood of Jesus speaks life over you. Through the blood of the lamb, ***you*** have the ability of Moses. You have the ability to stand face-to-face with the living God. You don't have to go to anyone else to get a revelation from him. God has made a way for you to approach him boldly, and it's through the blood of Jesus. This is the essence of the secret place.

Whether it's in the woods, on a mountaintop, in your bedroom, or in your break room at work, approach the secret place with the same reverence Moses did approaching the burning bush: "Take your sandals off your feet, for the place on which you are standing is holy ground" (Exodus 3:5). Make it a practice in your life to enter the secret place with the intention of encountering the Most High God. If there's one thing I've learned through meeting with Jesus, it's that he never denies a hungry heart.

Elijah came to the Lord hungry after a forty-day journey with no food. He was running for his life, and his hunger at this point was more for the word of the Lord than it was for food. Elijah is our second mountaintop seeker. Elijah hungered for the presence of the Lord, and the Lord did not leave him empty. After all his running, Elijah reached Mt. Sinai and made lodging in a cave. It was then that the Word of the Lord came to him, and this is what occurred:

"the LORD passed by, and a great and strong wind tore the mountains and broke in pieces the rocks before the LORD, but the LORD was not in the wind. And after the wind an earthquake, but the LORD was not in the earthquake. And after the earthquake a fire, but the LORD was not in the fire. And after the fire the sound of a low whisper." 1 Kings 19:11–12

What an amazing encounter with God. Can't you just imagine the wind rushing, the earth shaking, the mountain bursting into pieces, and flames ripping across the sky, just as a result of the passing of the Lord? What an amazing spectacle!

The focal point of this story comes after the displays of power. It is the still, gentle whisper. The scriptures go on to say that God himself was not in the exploding mountain, the fire, the earthquake, or the wind, but the Lord came directly in a still, gentle whisper.

Sometimes when the Lord shows up you get the wind of God. And his wind lifts us up to new heights! Sometimes when God shows up you get the fire of the Lord. The fire of God purifies our souls and ignites us for his glory. "Light me up Lord!" However, neither the wind nor the fire should be our pursuit if God is not directly in them. Don't get me wrong, we need the fire of God on our lives, we need *all* that the presence of the Lord brings, but we can't survive on fire and wind. We can't survive on the gifts of God, we can only survive off of *him, the bread of life.* Charles Spurgeon once said,

"This same lesson has to be learned over and over by us all: let us repeat it, 'Not by might, nor by power, but by my Spirit, saith the Lord.' It is to be lamented that the most of professors obstinately cling to the fatal error of looking for displays of power of one kind or another. I hear that a certain church is seeking for a very clever man: she thinks that God is in the wind... That still small voice will be hushed and silent, while the boastings of your wisdom resound like a howling wind or a thunder unaccompanied by rain.[25]"

It is possible for one's good gifts, such as the ability to preach well, to become too loud a wind for the whisper of the Holy Spirit to be heard. If your life is too loud, if your mind is too loud, if your ministry is too loud, you'll never be able to hear the still, gentle whisper of the Lord. The true, life changing power of God isn't found in great giftings or displays of power. It's found in the clarity of his voice. Faith itself comes by hearing, and hearing through the word of Christ.[26]

Go to the mountaintop now if you haven't yet today. Silence all other voices, including your cellphones. Wait patiently for God to speak to you. It's in the secret place that we put ourselves in a posture of hearing while waiting on the Lord, reading his word and praying. Open up you heart to the stillness of his voice. If you haven't met with him today, put this book down and find somewhere to meet with him intimately.

Intimacy is all God ever wanted with you. Don't settle for a religious show or man's agenda. Man's plan is to get you focused on the (do) of Christianity. Gods only

---

[25] The Complete Works of C. H. Spurgeon, Volume 28: Sermons 1637-1697
[26] Romans 10:17

trying to get you focused on the (who). His name is Jesus. He made you for himself. It's only from the (who) that we receive the true (do) of life.

Three days of fasting and prayer alone in the secret place could accomplish more than thirty years of hard work in ministry. God will always endorse his word and his name with the miraculous but if we would spend less time doing *"God's work"* and more time seeking God, we'd accomplish more in three years than in three lifetimes of striving in the flesh. *Get intimate with Jesus.* That is your purpose above all else in life.

You have God in the measure in which you desire Him. Only remember that the desire that brings God must be more than a feeble, fleeting wish. Wishing is one thing; willing is quite another. Lazily wishing and strenuously desiring are two entirely different postures of mind; the former gets nothing and the latter gets everything, gets God, and with God all that God can bring."

-*Alexander Maclaren*[27]

---

[27] The Homiletic Review, Volume 34 pg. 222

CHAPTER TWO

Church

The largest Christian revival in the history of the world is going on right now. It has been for decades. China, Africa, India, and South America have all been glowing with revival. China is currently the largest Christian nation in the world![1] I mean, there have been close to 200 million confessed salvations over the last few decades between Asia and Africa alone. Recently, a friend of mine went to Pakistan where he witnessed multitudes of Muslims turning to Christ like you wouldn't believe! The world is literally exploding with revival, and for some reason the United States of America is at the back of the pack.

    I believe this is partially because we've invented "church" outside the Bible's example of what church

---

[1] Research ancient China's "Shang Di, the Most High God." It will blow your mind. The God of the Bible is literally built into the ancient Chinese language.

actually is. If you knew nothing, sat down, read the Bible and believed it was actually God's word, your response wouldn't be to start a religion or build a massive church building. Actually, your response would look nothing like what the majority of American Christianity looks like. Churches all over America operate more like a big business, religious institution or a social club than a place of prayer and worship. Many churches in America start off spirit filled and hungry for the Lord but quickly become complacent and burn out. When "church" becomes a comfortable, religious routine the presence of God departs, and church services become empty and void. The natural response of man is to compensate for the void with a manufactured glory that mimics the true excitement of the presence of God. Ministry then becomes overwhelming and burdensome when *you* have to generate something each week.

The American Christian Church is absolutely desperate for Jesus, but they've forgotten the sound of his voice. They've forgotten what he looks like. They've forgotten what his touch feels like. They've forgotten his aroma. They have settled for man's production and have become defiant and numb to the Spirit of God who's only trying to lead them to back to Jesus. There is a massive wall built by man that rests in-between the people and Jesus, it needs to come down.

Gods true church can't be identified by any single denomination or church affiliation. The true church is sprinkled throughout them all like salt. Some denominations and churches have more salt than others. Some have none.

The original word for "church" used in the Greek was *ekklesia*. The word *ekklesia* is much more closely translated "group of people," "congregation," or "assembly" than "church." The way we use the word *church* nowadays can be directly credited to the narcissistic King James himself. He insisted his translators use the word *church* instead of *congregation* because he found it advantageous to make himself the head of the *church* opposed to the fully functioning, powerful body of Christ. Empowering the very people you want to control would not be a practical choice. King James did everything he could to limit the power of the *ekklesia*. Unfortunately, we see the same suppression happening in many churches across America today.

Jesus empowered the church by his Spirit for the expansion of his good news, his good works and most of all *himself*. Jesus didn't establish the church that most people are familiar with in America. The church Jesus established existed long before religious institutions took them over. Seeing church clearly is one of the biggest struggles we face in America. To see church clearly, we must see Jesus clearly. Jesus did not call us to hide in fancy buildings called churches. He called us to follow him, and in following him, we become his church.

> *"Jesus didn't call us to deliver sermons, he called us to deliver people"- Reinhard Bonnke*[28]

The true church is a preserved remnant who love Jesus intimately and live according to his word. Which means you can have church anywhere at any time as long as the church themselves are there. Don't get me wrong, the Bible gives plenty of structure and organization guidelines for how the church is to operate productively, but the church looks a whole lot different in other areas of the world where the remnant is growing at a much faster rate. The pastoral hierarchy in America often looks very similar to the pyramid of power we see in the Vatican. Pastors are supposed to be servants of the flock, building and lifting them up to be sent out. In America many pastors are exalted and lifted up like the Pope within their own church. This is completely backwards to the lifestyle of Jesus,

> *"even as the Son of Man came not to be served but to serve, and to give his life as a ransom for many."*[29]

I was recently conversing with a Christian medical

---

[28] *Reinhard Bonnke* December 9, 1986
[29] Matthew 20:28

doctor from India who has now planted over 40,000 churches in India. I asked him how he was so successful at planting churches. He responded with a question, "Do you know how many rabbits you can bread from two parent rabbits over the course of seven years?" I knew they bred quickly, so I said, "I don't know thirty thousand?" He said, "Not even close. Nearly two hundred billion." Then he asked me, "Do you know how many elephants you can get in seven years with two parent elephants?" I guessed something like ten. He said, "Only three."

"Michael," he went on to say, "the key to church reproduction in India is that we don't try to build elephant churches; we try to build rabbit churches. In America, you typically build elephant churches, and elephant churches take a lot of money and resources to run. It's this slow-moving process that keeps their reproduction so slow. In India, we equip the body of Christ to raise up leaders to start other churches, most of which are held in people's homes and don't take much if any money to run. We start a church, build up leaders, send them out, and the process continues."

This model of church growth looks much more Holy Spirit lead and biblical than what we see in a lot of America today. It makes you wonder, what's more important to the average American church leader: the advancement of the gospel or the money, power and control that comes with running a big operation church? Don't get me wrong, there are several big operation churches and ministries that are extremely fruitful in the United States.

Overall, it's not about the size or bank account of the church or ministry, but the heart of the church or ministry and its ultimate direction and purpose.

Unfortunately, in America, spreading the gospel at the most productive rate is not in a lot of churches budgets. In a congregation of even 300 people, you have to question how many people have the pastoral gifting that are never built up to use it. I believe there have been Billy Graham–level evangelists who never stepped into their calling because they weren't built up to *GO*, but they were discipled to stay. The thought process of the typical American church is, "We only need one or two pastors, so why don't you stack chairs or get on the ushering team." Serving is a vital gift, and I'm not devaluing it. We all need to be servants first. Jesus washed his disciples' feet. But how many pastors, teachers, evangelists, apostles, and prophets watch their lives go by sitting in Sunday service every week never being built up and equipped for the mission field? Many churches train their congregations to get as many people in the church doors as possible so the pastor can get them "saved" on Sunday. It's great to bring the unsaved to church, however, the pastor should really be equipping his congregation to preach the gospel themselves and encouraging them to *GO* and make disciples. We are all called to do the work of an evangelist![30]

There is a treacherous "church machine" in America that has been built out of the depravity of man.

---

[30] 2 Timothy 4:5

The machine takes a lot of money and maintenance to stay moving. The machine is more focused on advancing its territory than building up the body of Christ. The machines software calculates raised hands as salvations. The machine keeps preaching Gods word to plow the way for its own agenda. The machine detects a true move of God and claims it for itself by branding it. The machine runs off of the approval of man. The machine creates an atmosphere and labels it *Holy Spirit*. The machine creates its own hype and calls it *Revival*. The machine does not know it's a machine, for its double minded in all it does.

Most of the machine's efforts are spent maintaining itself. Be very aware of the great American church machine. Do not be seduced by its slick appearance, feel good messages and mass approval ratings.

Do not settle for anything less than the presence of the living God.

There have been amazing things happening in America where the remnant is uniting but imagine how much more fruitful the Christian church would be as a whole if we'd stop *doing* church and actually started *being* the true church Christ called us to be. Our gathering together as the church should be a place where we can come to edify one another and pour out unto God in unity. This can only happen when the believers are personally being filled during the week in their alone time with God. However, many times, believers are not being filled personally during the week because they were taught to come "get filled" each Sunday at church. The church machine methods need to be abandoned. It's our only hope of seeing true revival. We need a mighty remnant led by mighty men to stand up, count everything but Jesus as loss, and lead the way. A lukewarm church will not be able to stay standing in these last days. The books of Philemon, Romans and Colossians speak of house churches. The book of Corinthians speaks of bigger churches. Your church model is going to be different according to the Holy Spirits call on your local church's life. The church size or location isn't the important thing. We should always be multiplying and peacefully dividing. The heartbeat of your church is what matters. It's time to rethink church entirely. It's time to be the church God intended us to be. A unified remnant, steadfast with one shared goal in mind: *Max capacity Kingdom advancement.*

For it is time for judgment to begin at the household of God; and if it begins with us, what will be the outcome for those who do not obey the gospel of God? 1 Peter 4:17

Mighty Men /New Wine

A Christ like father figure is extremely important to have in life yet incredibly rare to come by. Especially for children in America where nearly half the population is born to unwed parents and more than a quarter of the population doesn't have any father figure at all in their life. God has shown us what the perfect Father looks like in himself and what the perfect man looks like through his Son Jesus. I believe that the steady decline of mighty men in America is the core reason for the decay of our society. Just a few godly men can transform an entire nation. King David and his mighty men are perhaps the greatest example of this.

David was a man after God's own heart (Acts 13:22). What set him apart was years of intimacy with the Lord. David was a shepherd long before he was a king. It was the history that David developed with God in the secret place that shaped him into the mighty man of God that would rule over Israel. As a shepherd, David developed trust in the Lord to carry him through difficult situations. He killed a lion and a bear long before ever having the faith in God to take down Goliath. What made David so mighty was his reliance on God, not his own strength.

"Not by might, nor by power, but by my Spirit, says

the LORD of hosts."[31]

David didn't force himself out of the wilderness, he was called out of the wilderness. David didn't force himself onto the throne before God put him there because David didn't desire the throne, he desired the Lord. We live in a world where everyone wants the throne. What most don't realize is that the highest throne is at the feet of Jesus. If you want to go high for the Lord, you must go low. Enter into the wilderness with assurance that God is doing a work in you like he was doing in David in the fields. You don't want to miss out on the history that God wants to develop with you in this season. Don't be in a rush to get to the place you think you should be. God wants to slowly develop your character through trials. When we truly learn to trust in the Lord through our trials, he always shows himself faithful just as he did to David.

It took nearly two decades for David to move from shepherd to king. God wants to know; will you be faithful with the little? Will you be steadfast when no one is watching? Where is your heart?

"There are many of us that are willing to do great things for the Lord, but few of us are willing to do little things."

-D.L. Moody

---

[31] Zechariah 4:6

Humility was David's greatest quality. David was a man of war who often played the harp, danced and wept before the Lord. He was chosen and anointed to be king, but never sought to exalt himself above King Saul. Even when he had the perfect chance. Eventually, God lifted David up. David became king after Saul's pride lead him to his own death.

One of the main reasons that David was such a successful king was because he didn't just rely on his own God given strength or his own God given knowledge. He always had other mighty men of God around him to consult with.

> *"Where there is no guidance, a people falls, but in an abundance of counselors there is safety."* [32]

> *"Without counsel plans fail, but with many advisers they succeed."* [33]

David knew that without counsel plans fail. David had a council of thirty-seven mighty men around him all the time. These were no ordinary "yes-men" that David bossed around. Each one of David's mighty men was empowered by God with amazing capabilities in battle. Just one of these men was capable of taking down 300 men on his own and another even 800. One of them fought so valiantly in

---

[32] Proverbs 11:14
[33] Proverbs 15:22

battle he wasn't able to unclench his hand from his sword after the war was over. *This is how we should be today with our sword, the Word of God* (Ephesians 6:17). Many men would feel threatened by a group of such powerful men. However, David was humble and confident in who he was in God. So, this powerful fellowship was able to conquer *together*.

I want you to imagine these men in today's world. These men would be considered a powerhouse group for the kingdom of God—some prophets, some pastor-teachers, some evangelists, and some apostles, all equipped for spreading the gospel and destroying the works of the enemy. Nothing could stop David and his mighty men. Nothing could stop a group of Spirit-filled, spiritually gifted men such as this today.

The main reason we don't see many spiritual armies like this in America today is because there is a sheer lack of mighty men. Most men don't want to pay the price it takes to become a mighty man of God. The cost is too high for them to lose all they desire of the world. Many men become mighty in their own eyes, which fills them with competitive pride toward each other. Instead of seeing each other as an asset they see each other as a threat to their own throne. Instead of uniting in great council for great war strategy we are comparing whose ministry is stronger. Our own insecurities are keeping us from a powerful remnant assembly of counsel. I truly believe thirty-seven humble, mighty men led by the Holy Spirit could transform New England from a land of "frozen chosen" to a land flowing with new wine. "New wine" biblically represents the outpouring of the Holy Spirit.

There is a resistance against new wine, for the old wine has spoiled the stomach of the church for decades. It is as Luke 5:39 says, "No one after drinking old wine desires new, for he says, 'The old is good.'" Old wine is poured out of old wineskins. Old wineskins are the old religious methods of Christianity that have stretched and decayed from generations of man's manipulation. These old wineskins are full of wine that has spoiled and gone sour. New wine is a reality. I believe very soon fresh wine is going to be poured out over America, but as of right now, fresh wine would burst the decayed wineskins of many churches.

"Neither is new wine put into old wineskins. If it is, the skins burst and the wine is spilled and the skins are destroyed. But new wine is put into fresh wineskins, and so both are preserved." Matthew 9:17

Four hundred years ago, God preserved a remnant out of Europe. This remnant was abandoning the old corrupted wineskins of religion in Europe. God was preparing new wineskins in the New World. God led the remnant of 1620 across the Atlantic on a wine ship called the Mayflower. Yes, the Mayflower was a *wine ship*! However, the Mayflower was never designed to cross the

Atlantic but only built to go from port to port in Europe. This wine ship was bringing new wine to the New World, not in bottles but in temples of the Holy Spirit! I believe new wineskins are being developed in America and more specifically in New England once again.

In order for this new wineskin to go forth, it is going to take a unified generation that is hungry for Jesus and filled with the Spirit of God. At first this new wineskin might crush church attendance numbers by 50 percent. The uncompromised truth of the word is something a lot of people don't want to hear:

> "For the time is coming when people will not endure sound teaching, but having itching ears they will accumulate for themselves teachers to suit their own passions, and will turn away from listening to the truth and wander off into myths." 2 Timothy 4:3–4

We must not fall subject to preaching messages that suit the sinful desires of man. We must not be persuaded by numbers or the approval of man. Many churches have an appearance of godliness but deny his power. It will not be the preaching that ushers in new wine but the life changing action upon the truth. Engaging and changing is a lot different than sitting and listening. We must purify the church from the sin of the world and preach the full truth of God's word once again:

> "But now I am writing to you not to associate with anyone who bears the name of brother if he is guilty of sexual immorality or greed, or is an idolater, reviler, drunkard, or swindler—not even to eat with such a one. For what have I to do with judging outsiders? Is it not those inside the church whom you are to judge? God judges those outside. "Purge the evil person from among you."
>
> 1 Corinthians 5:11–13

When's the last time your pastor told you to purge the evil person from among you? Do we take God's word seriously? We don't need any more halfhearted, lukewarm believers dragging down the rest of the body. We need mighty men and women of God! Twelve mighty men full of the Spirit are more prosperous and effective for the kingdom of God than ten million lukewarm, halfhearted "Christians". We need bold, selfless men who aren't worried about appearance, money, church numbers, or platforms. Men who will sow for themselves righteousness and break the fallow grounds of sin, dead religion and man's agenda. "Sow for yourselves righteousness; reap steadfast love; break up your fallow ground, for it is the time to seek the LORD, that he may come and rain righteousness upon you" (Hosea 10:12). We always hear about the seed that fell on bad soil, but are we willing to do what it takes to break that soil up and make it fertile so seeds can grow in it? Tilled soil and new wineskins are perhaps one in the same.

King Saul had many great victories and achievements attached to his name. All of which were overshadowed by his disobedience and pride. As God anointed and raised up Saul's humble servant David to take his place, Saul attempted to kill David multiple times instead of rightfully build him up. This same spirit of Saul is suppressing the church today in America. The spirit of Saul is hindering the same church it's trying to lead. The spirit of Saul is threatened by mighty David's who are rising up. The Saul's of this nation will not release, build up, or send out the anointed. They only look to suppress them and demand their elegance. Just as David played the harp over Saul and Saul was delivered from torment, so too will this David generation bring healing to its elders.

In the Old Testament the *Ark of the Covenant* represented the manifest glory and presence of God on earth. Saul lost the *Ark of the Covenant* due to his disobedience and pride. The first thing king David did when he took the throne was go after the *Ark*! Today in America it is up to the mighty men of God to retrieve the Ark once again! The mighty men know we are *NOTHING* without the *manifest presence* of God! The Saul leaders are falling, and new wineskins are being developed. The mighty men of God will show the world what being a great leader and father looks like, building up, nurturing, and sending out more mighty men to take territory for the kingdom of God.

We need mighty men to show us what a true heart cry looks like. You'll be challenged to give up everything to receive his anointing. Remember, God is seeking hearts. He's not looking for religion, programs, platforms or social media followers. God only wants your heart!

"For the eyes of the LORD run to and fro throughout the whole earth, to give strong support to those whose heart is fully devoted toward him. You have done foolishly in this..." 2 Chronicles 16:9

Whoever the Lord gives strong support to will be victorious. I guarantee it! This is a trumpet blast for the next generation. Rise up, mighty men and women of God! Lead the next generation to the heart of Jesus through the power of the Holy Spirit!

The Remnant

After a great display of the Lord's power was shown to Elijah on Mt. Sinai, Elijah heard a still, gentle whisper of the Lord. The gentle whisper asked Elijah what he was doing there. Elijah responded,

> "I have been very jealous for the LORD, the God of hosts. For the people of Israel have forsaken your covenant, thrown down your altars, and killed your prophets with the sword, and I, even I only, am left, and they seek my life, to take it away." 1 Kings 19:10

Elijah has an encounter with the living God and all he has to say is, *"God, I'm jealous for you!"* Elijah's heart is clearly devoted to the Lord. This is the same heart cry that the Lord is developing in the remnant of America today. Elijah told God he was jealous, or zealous, for him and that he was angry the people of Israel had abandoned their faith in him. God then informed Elijah that there were still 7,000 righteous left in Israel. What a relief that must have been to hear. Elijah was assuming that all was lost, but the Lord told him that his labor was not in vain, that a remnant still remained.

I love how the apostle Paul expounds on this account of Elijah hundreds of years later:

"God has not rejected his people whom he foreknew. Do you not know what the Scripture says of Elijah, how he appeals to God against Israel?...But what is God's reply to him? "I have kept for myself seven thousand men who have not bowed the knee to Baal." So too at the present time there is a remnant, chosen by grace."[34]

Paul was saying that even during his time, hundreds of years later, there was still a remnant that remained steadfast for the Lord. I believe this scripture applies today as well. In this present time, there is a remnant chosen by grace. The remnant today might feel like Elijah. Alone with the world seeking their life. *Do not be discouraged!* There is a strong remnant that remains all over the world. There may be fewer than ever before in America but they're still here.

When the Jews returned to the promised land under Zerubbabel, they totaled around 2% of the entire Jewish population that was in slavery in Babylon. That means 98% of the people chose to stay in the comfort of Babylon. They didn't mind being slaves. I know this may seem shocking to some, but I believe the remnant in America today could be as few as 2% of all self-identified Christians. We are to flee from sin and be slaves to righteousness, but I believe the majority of church goers are happy with the comforts and pleasures of Babylon and could care less about fleeing their sinful slavery.

God will use the 2%! He has before and he will do it again!

A generation of mountaintop seekers who hear God's voice is being birthed. God is raising up a remnant army for the last days in America. An army that will

---

[34] Romans 11:2,4-5

worship him in spirit and in truth. A people like the prophet Samuel who will learn to discern the Lord's voice from the voice of the world because their lives are entirely dedicated to God. A generation of uncompromising spiritual mothers and fathers who are jealous for the Lord and will consecrate their children to Him, raising them in the way they should go. The birthing of this generation is happening as we speak.

The remnant of America is preserving our country from the ashes of Sodom and Gomorrah. There are many sons of Israel that scatter the earth. Even more so today that have been grafted in by the grace of the Father, but only a remnant of them will be saved. For the Lord will carry out his sentence upon the earth fully and without delay.

> And Isaiah cries out concerning Israel: "Though the number of the sons of Israel be as the sand of the sea, only a remnant of them will be saved, for the Lord will carry out his sentence upon the earth fully and without delay." And as Isaiah predicted,
>
> "If the Lord of hosts had not left us offspring,
>   we would have been like Sodom
>   and become like Gomorrah." Romans 9:27–29

God is always with his people and he consistently preserves a remnant, even if it's only eight people on a ship with a bunch of animals. The remnants way is not popular because the path they've chosen is not like the worlds, it is narrow, and few will find it. However, hidden in the vineyard of America there is a path with new wine ready to flow through Gods true sons and daughters.

> Thus says the LORD:
>
> "As the new wine is found in the cluster, and they say, 'Do not destroy it, for there is a blessing in it,' so I will do for my servants' sake, and not destroy them all."[35]

There is a blessing in the cluster! Do not destroy it! Just like the wheats and the tares, we cannot remove the tare because we would harm the wheat. Do not destroy the cluster because amongst the sour, spoiled, rotten grapes there are pure remnant grapes ready to burst fresh with new wine!

> "And it shall be as when the reaper gathers standing grain and his arm harvests the ears, and as when one gleans the ears of grain in the Valley of Rephaim. Gleanings will be left in it, as when an olive tree is beaten— two or three berries in the top of the highest bough, four or five on the branches of a fruit tree, declares the LORD God of Israel."[36]

God is beating and shaking the olive tree of

---

[35] Isaiah 65:8
[36] Isaiah 17:5-6

America. Only his remnant will withstand the sifting of his staff. The harvest of the last days is upon us. But only those who are *wholly* devoted to the Lord will inherit the kingdom of God. The weeds will be left and tossed into the fire (Matthew 13:40). *The Remnant* are those who are *wholly* devoted to the Lord. Just like the earthly *Promised Land* of Gods people Israel, we must understand that the eternal Promised Land to come is only for those who have chosen to *wholly* follow the Lord.

> "'Surely none of the men who came up out of Egypt, from twenty years old and upward, shall see the land that I swore to give to Abraham, to Isaac, and to Jacob, because they have not wholly followed me, none except Caleb the son of Jephunneh the Kenizzite and Joshua the son of Nun, for they have *wholly* followed the LORD.' And the LORD's anger was kindled against Israel, and he made them wander in the wilderness forty years, until all the generation that had done evil in the sight of the Lord was gone." Numbers 32:11–13

This was the remnant preservation of 1552BC. God was filtering out the true remnant of his people and he is doing the same thing throughout the world today. We must choose to *wholly* devote our hearts and our lives to the Lord. It's going to cost you everything. Jesus must become your everything. There is no room for the compromised heart in the Promised Land. You must choose now. The last days are upon us.

With all love, humility and unity.

Join the harvest.

Join *The Remnant*.

The Way

The Way is mentioned many times in the book of Acts as the lifestyle of the first church. This was not just a sect of Judaism but truly a way of life structured upon Jesus himself and his ministry. This is "The Way" we desperately need to return to in America. Jesus himself said, "I am the way" (John 14:6). Even more so, 1 John 2:6 says, "whoever says he abides in him ought to walk in the same way in which he walked." There are many false versions of "The Way." There's even a cult named *The Way*. The true way of Jesus is not some mystical thing. The way has been mapped out clearly for us and our forefathers for centuries in God's word.

When the remnant of 1620 landed in Plymouth, Massachusetts, they made camp next to a river so when spring came, thousands of fish began to swim from the ocean into the river. What an amazing providential blessing to have food for months that can be salted and preserved just swim right to you. The fish the Pilgrims caught in this river are called herring. Herring predominantly live in the ocean. However, they are born in freshwater rivers and ponds. They swim back to the river they came from once a year to lay eggs in the very ponds and rivers they were born in. This mystery has had scientists marveling for centuries. No one seems to know how the fish can travel miles into the ocean and find their way back to the same pond they came from. The truth is, God told us hundreds of years ago how these fish navigate the ocean. The mystery is in the path:

"the birds of the heavens, and the fish of the sea, whatever passes along the paths of the seas."[37]

Psalm chapter eight speaks of the majesty of the Lord and how he gave man dominion over all the earth. He describes plainly that there are pathways in the sea. Whatever these pathways look like to sea life is unknown and specific to their kind. God created many other pathways, some for the birds in the sky and some for the bugs in the ground. All living things have their own pathways with their own distinct purpose and direction.

God made the perfect pathway for his most loved creation (mankind) and it's called the pathway of *life*. This pathway is readily accessible today, but sin has created

---

[37] Psalm 8:8

another pathway for mankind and its name is *death*. God pleads with us in his word to choose *life,* but something keeps drawing the vast majority of mankind down the path of *death*.

Imagine you are going for a hike through the woods with a group of friends. You're hiking along a path when all of a sudden you run into two gates that block off two different pathways. One path is narrow and looks rather difficult to hike, and the other is wide open and easy. There's something that doesn't feel right about the easy path, so you pull out your map, and it clearly shows you that the easy path is full of quicksand and lethal snakes and its end is a giant lava pit. You try to show your friends. You say, "Hey, guys, look at this map. There's no way we should go down that path. It's full of destruction, and its end is inevitable death." But they don't believe you. They just insist, "Who would want to go down that difficult narrow path when you could just go down this easy wide path?" They joke about your map, and they say they don't believe it. They even gang up against you and start making fun of you. They depart from you, head down the wide path, and you never see them again.

> "Enter by the narrow gate. For the gate is wide and the way is easy that leads to destruction, and those who enter by it are many. For the gate is narrow and the way is hard that leads to life, and those who find

it are few."[38]

Grace is inscribed above the narrow gate. Its path is very difficult, and there are few who choose it. But what most people don't realize is when you enter the narrow gate you're suddenly not alone anymore. The Holy Spirit joins you on your journey. He is the one who helps you on the narrow path. He is your guide and your comforter. The narrow path's final destination is *life*. The Spirit reminds you that **salvation is to the one who overcomes**[39]. The final destination of the wide, easy path is *death*. Many choose this path because they are persuaded by the inscription above the wide gate that says *Pleasure*.

If you choose the pathway of life, and I pray you do, the enemy cannot overtake you if you stay on the narrow path. If you resist the devil, he will flee from you. The enemy does not know where the narrow path goes, for it is a path of wisdom and life. He cannot see what is not his. The narrow path is just as invisible to him as the fish's path in the sea is to you.

I think the King James Version of the Bible puts it best in Job 28:7–8:

"There is a path which no fowl knoweth, and which the vulture's eye hath not seen: The lion's whelps have not trodden it, nor the fierce lion passed by it."

---

[38] Matthew 7:13-14
[39] Revelation 2 & 3

This scripture is talking about the narrow path. The enemy, who is like a vulture and a lion seeking someone to devour, has no power over you when you are walking the narrow path. David said, by the word of God's lips he avoided the paths of the violent. Therefore, it is only when you choose to step off the narrow path that you can truly be overtaken.

God will guide you along the narrow path. His word is a lamp unto our feet (Psalm 119:105). Sometimes we get anxious because we want to see what's a mile ahead of us. God is only giving light to our feet because he wants us to develop dependency on him.

Dependency develops intimacy.

It's only by depending entirely on him for light that we are led in the right direction. If we could see more, we'd run off without God and find ourselves in trouble.

Joseph was sold into slavery to preserve a remnant of Gods people in Egypt. If it wasn't for Joseph's slavery in Egypt, his bloodline would have been tarnished by the Canaanites or starved out by famine. This path didn't look like *life* to Joseph when he was sold into slavery, but we must remember while on the narrow path Gods ways are not our ways and that "there is a way that seems right to a man, but its end is the way to death."[40]

---

40 Proverbs 14:12

So, whether the narrow path makes sense to you or not, "Trust in the Lord with all your heart, and do not lean on your own understanding.

"In all your ways acknowledge him, and he will make straight your paths" Proverbs 3:5–6

Acknowledge means to admit the existence and/or truth of something. So, admit the existence of God and his truth in everything that you do, and he will make straight your paths.

It's only by knowing *The Way* personally that you'll be able to stay on this narrow path. He's given us everything we need for this life's journey in himself.

Thank you, Jesus!

Identity Crisis

You find your confidence in whatever you identify as. You find your identity in wherever you pull your confidence from. Everyone wants to be confident in who they are. No matter what social or financial demographic people are in, they find their identity in something and then extract their confidence from that identification. Mankind is desperate to find their identity.

Motorcyclists often group up and identify as bikers. They feel confident when they "roll out" together. "Models" who flaunt their half-naked bodies or walk around wearing provocative clothing find confidence in causing people to admire or lust after their looks. I grew up with a lot of "tough guys" who found their confidence in putting fear in people. A lot of people turn to the LGBTTQQIAAP group solely for the purpose of finding their identity. They'll keep adding letters until everyone feels confident about their identity within that group.

Several generations have recently found their confidence in their social media image, and many people identify with the fake people that they portray themselves as on social media. A lot of people just want to be rich. They identify with their bank accounts, and their confidence is built on how many zeros are attached to their name. This way of thinking even creeps into the Christian church!

Many Christians still have an orphan spirit. They try to find their confidence in the approval from man through Christian ministry. Who am I? What's my calling? What will my platform be?

I'm here to tell you today that if you identify as *anything* other than CHILD OF GOD[41] you need to shed

---

[41] This includes all biblical identities in Christ including *bride of Christ*

yourself of that self-image and identification right now.

Jesus is the *image* of the invisible God. The only image you are supposed to find your confidence in is Jesus! God made you in *his* image, and when you identify as a child of God you no longer find your confidence in *self*, but your confidence is in Christ Jesus!

Those of you struggling with anxiety, this is a healing remedy. Die to self and self-image! Leave *you* at the cross. *You* don't exist anymore. Your life now consists of Jesus living through you. Anxiety itself often comes on as extreme self-awareness. How can anxiety exist within self when *self* no longer exists? When *self* truly dies, anxiety dies with it. If you ever try to revive *self*, anxiety will be revived with it. Anxiety is often a malfunction from doing something you were never designed to do. Like trying to drive a boat on land. It's not going to work properly or at all. You can't function properly outside of the Great Engineer's purpose for your life. We were created to be upwardly focused worshipers of the Most High God. Any other identification is focused downwardly and aimed to receive the approval of man.

I want this truth to be poured out on your head like oil. You don't have to become something or someone! Let go of who you once thought you were. Let go! Cry, "Abba, Father!" In all humility reach out your arms and receive his sweet embrace. He's waiting to adopt you, child. He gave up everything so you could give up everything and receive everything in him. His yoke is easy, and his burden is light, in him you don't have to be heavy laden to make something of yourself.

Christ is the reward. In him the fullness of God dwells bodily[42]. Jesus is who you were made for. Jesus is the one whom your soul longs for. Stop looking for fulfillment in all the wrong places. Jesus weeps over his lost sheep. He rejoices over his prodigal children.

When you receive adoption from God, you no longer have the fears of an orphan: Where will I sleep? What will I eat? Who will take care of me? Does anyone love me? Will I ever have a family? What do people think of me? When you receive sonship in Christ the anxiety of identification dissipates. There is nothing more freeing in life than letting go of everything you thought you once were and receiving the newness of life in Jesus. That is what being born again truly represents. That's why I don't encourage people to be baptized until they're really at this point of letting go. In baptism, you and your *self-image* go down under water and never come back up. *CHILD OF GOD* arises out of the water in freedom in Christ Jesus.

"I have been crucified with Christ. It is no longer I who live, but Christ who lives in me. And the life I now live in the flesh I live by faith in the Son of God, who loved me and gave himself for me." Galatians 2:20

---

[42] Colossians 2:9

Thank you, Jesus! Thank you, Father, for adopting me! Thank you for your promised Holy Spirit! I'm so grateful I don't have to amount to anything in my own strength. All my confidence is found in you, Daddy[43]!

Influencer

There is an epidemic that has plagued Christianity over the last 10 years. Pop culture and social media have left their DNA footprint on the "Christian world". Young Christians are growing up in a society that says, "having massive influence is success." That the number of followers you have defines your success. How many views did you get? How many people follow your brand? How many likes, views or shares did you get? My brothers and sisters, this is a toxic poison we have to purge from the body of Christ.

Many influential self-proclaimed Christians will stand before God and say Lord, Lord! Don't you recall all that I did in your name? I had millions of followers! I moved mountains! I had great influence! God will say to many, depart from me I never knew you, workers of lawlessness.[44] The question is,

---

[43] *Abba* is closer to *Daddy* in Hebrew than simply *father*.
[44] Authors paraphrase of Matthew 7:23

Does God know you?

Knowing Jesus is the focal point of your existence. It's from the place of intimacy that God will use you in the capacity that he desires. If your influence on others is not coming from a place of knowing Jesus, you'll manufacture his substance and sell a counterfeit savior. Counterfeits have no value or substance to them. What has more value? A 24k gold bar or a spray-painted gold stack of bricks.

It's not about the size of the circle you have influence on. It's about the density of Christ you have to pour out onto them. Does the influence you carry contain the genuine substance and richness of the Lord or does your influence contain a manufactured synthetic mix of programs and self?

Does God trust you with his presence?

On my own I have absolutely nothing to offer anyone. I need the density of Jesus to flow through me if I'm going to truly benefit anyone. I'd rather pour a gallon of water on one person that's burning than flick a drop of water on ten million burning people. We are called to make disciples. Making disciples is an intimate and costly sacrifice of leading people to the feet of Jesus. If we are going to extinguish the fire of hell that is coming for the people, we have to make sure that we are pulling from the well that never runs dry. That well is no other than Christ Jesus himself.

What well are you pulling your water from?

Christian, if you want to have influence for the Lord, start by living like Jesus! I see many mainstream "Christian influencers" influencing the world for a God that they clearly don't even know! Jesus said, if you want to go high, you must go low[45]. Stop conforming to the patterns of this world and defining your self-worth by man's approval.

The influence Jesus had on the world was a result of his closeness to the Father. The influence the disciples had on the earth was a result of their closeness to Jesus.

The seven sons of Sceva in Acts chapter 19 were men of influence. Their father was a Jewish high priest. These young men were some of the top influencers of their day. One day they attempted to cast out demons in the name of Jesus, but they were unsuccessful and overthrown. Their influence didn't extend into the supernatural. The demons said they knew Jesus and even recognized the name of Paul. These men however were unknown by the demons and carried no authority over them. *These men weren't affiliated with God.* They weren't pulling their water from Jesus. They were pulling their water from their own cisterns of self-promotion.

These men only knew *of* Jesus. They didn't know Jesus personally. When you know Jesus and Jesus knows you, Jesus will show himself strongly on your behalf, because you're his friend. When demons encountered the

---

[45] Authors paraphrase of Matthew 18:4

apostles of Jesus they fled like cowards because they didn't operate in their own authority but rather the authority of Jesus who was *with them always*[46].

There's a wave of Christian influencers who use "positive influence" as a means of building up their own brand or movement. By simply "helping others better themselves" they gain more followers and stretch their territory of influence. The apostle Paul talked about this in Philippians chapter one. People will use the gospel as a means to promote self through a smokescreen of "benefiting others." They do this by pacifying people who believe that the mark of a good leader is someone who puffs up his followers like a balloon. These influencers always try to make you feel good about yourself. They promise you hope and shower you with optimism. These influencers always act super excited to see you and they'll clothe you with flattery and insincere praise. It's as if they stick a balloon pump in your ear and don't stop pumping until your head explodes. This is not the mark of a good leader. This looks nothing at all like the way Jesus edified and built up his disciples.

When celebrities come to put their faith in Jesus, some Christians seem to lose their minds over this. They think, "wow, Jesus is going to use that person's name and influence to make himself famous." *News flash,* Jesus doesn't need your name or your fame! He already has the name that is above every other name! He takes no name

---

[46] Matthew 28:20

farmer boys and turns them into world changing evangelists.

Being known by man has zero value on its own! Being known by man carries zero power! Desire to be known by God!

Men who are known by God have influence in heaven that transcends to earth. Abraham pleaded with the Lord over Sodom and Gomorrah and saved righteous Lot. Joshua prayed and the earth stood still. Elijah called down fire from heaven to destroy his adversaries. Moses parted the Red Sea and Peter raised the dead. These are the type of men I want to be around. This is the circle that I want influencing me! Men who influence the heart of God!

Check your circle!

Check the circle of people that have influence on you! If it's not a circle of people on their hands and knees at the feet of Jesus, you need to find another circle. I've watched men with great potential get extinguished by joining circles that are pursuing the vanities of this world in the name of "Jesus." It's vitally important to surround yourself with people who love Jesus more than you do. This leads to the question that will shape your life forever.

Is Jesus the means for you to get other things or is he himself the one thing?

Are you using Jesus? Many come to Jesus for what they can get out of him. Jesus is humble enough to entertain these guests for a while with love. However, to truly follow him, *HE* must become *EVERYTHING* to you. If you follow Jesus to get a healthy lifestyle, spouse, family, house, platform, career, notability, money, peace of mind, comfort, pleasure… you're putting these things above Jesus. You will miss the *one thing* and your life's treasures will disintegrate into ashes at the coming judgment of the Lord.

Influence that doesn't point people to the feet of Jesus has zero value. You want to add value to someone's life? Teach them how to submit to and obey the living word of God. Teach them how to find all that they need at the feet of Jesus. Influence people to die to themselves, pick up their cross and follow Jesus. However, you must get to that place first! You can only take people to places you have been yourself! You can only lead people to the feet of Jesus if you're there daily.

Your business, your brand, your logo, your name, your ministry, your platform, your circle of influence, will all burn up. What remains is the only thing that ever mattered.

Your influence in heaven.

Does God know you?

Revival

"God would never give the mantle of revival to a man until he doesn't want it anymore"[47] *– Carter Conlon*

Do you want to be used by God or do you want to be *seen* being used by God? If God gave the platform of revival to those who desire it, revival would quickly become a top achievement on their resume. The pride of man is hungry for power and acknowledgement. If we desire the mantle of revival, we desire to be elevated with or above God. This desire is a deceptive abomination that leads many into the numbers game of ministry. The platform of revival is going to fall into the hands of a people who desire lowlines, not a mantle. A people who desire the one who went lower than any before or after him, Christ Jesus.

Jesus said his Father's house should be a house of prayer (Matthew 21:13). That is, prayer should be the church's main function. Sadly, it's a whole lot easier to talk about, preach on, and study the topic of prayer than it is to actually get people to pray. I've heard it said, "If you want to know how much your church loves the pastor, do a headcount on Sunday morning. If you want to know how much your church loves God, count how many people are

---

[47] TSC: A Prayer Meeting Outside of Sodom, October 27, 2019, Carter Conlon

at the weekly prayer meeting." I wouldn't say that's entirely accurate, but the point is clear: the value of prayer has heavily diminished within the church.

The entire United States used to fast and pray collectively as a nation. Then somewhere along the line we forgot what Jesus said, "You can do nothing apart from me"[48]. The definition of nothing is "no thing; not anything; naught."[1] I'm not being facetious; I'm just making the point clear. Church services would be so much more productive if we cried out to the Lord in thanksgiving, praise and prayer for two hours rather than sit back reclined listening to the pastor's sermon while checking social media and updates of the game on our phones. Church has become a consumer product opposed to a joint effort in pursuing and glorifying God.

If your church isn't a praying church, it's a dead church. Jesus could have said his Father's house was a house of teaching, gathering, studying, fellowship or giving, but he made it clear that it was to be a house of prayer, because he knew that without fervent prayer, we can do absolutely nothing!

Prayer should be mingled with praise. I have heard that in New England after the Puritans had settled there a

---

[48] (John 15:5, author's paraphrase).
[1] *Dictionary.com*, s.v. "nothing," accessed July 3, 2019, www.dictionary.com/browse/nothing.

long while, they used to have very often a day of humiliation, fasting, and prayer, till they had so many days of fasting, humiliation, and prayer, that at last a good senator proposed that they should change it for once, and have a day of thanksgiving. (Spurgeon)[49]

There has been a lot of talk about revival in the Christian communities of America lately. A lot of what is said is prophetic and encouraging but a lot of what is said is just hype from ministries looking for opportunities to expand their growth. As encouraging as it might be to see the conservatives of America uniting by the hundreds of thousands to end abortion and fight against the radical left. This is not revival! Revival is when a nation gets on their face before the Lord and repents of their sin. This has to start with the church! The Lord is looking for the revival of *HIS* people. The church is in bondage, the chains on the church need to be broken!

True revival will only happen through sincere, humble, repentant, heart cry prayer. That is why the staple verse of this book is:

"If my people who are called by my name humble themselves, and pray and seek my face and turn from their wicked ways, then I will hear from heaven and will forgive

---

[49] The Metropolitan Tabernacle Pulpit, Volume 7 pg.55

their sin and heal their land." 2 Chronicles 7:14

In the books of 2 Kings and Isaiah we see a clear example of what sincere prayer for revival looks like. Hezekiah, the king of Judah, heard the words of his enemy Sennacherib, king of Assyria. They are blasphemous words with intent to attack. In this context Assyria represents a dark cloud of evil, destruction, confusion, and spiritual oppression. Sennacherib says through his mouthpiece, the *Rabshakeh*,

> "Do not listen to Hezekiah, for thus says the king of Assyria: 'Make your peace with me and come out to me. Then each one of you will eat of his own vine, and each one of his own fig tree, and each one of you will drink the water of his own cistern."[50]

Sennacherib is promoting the god of *self*, seducing people into being their own gods, eating from their own vines, eating their own fruit, and drinking from their own cisterns. The vine, fruit, and cistern are all things of God, and it is no coincidence that Sennacherib is attributing these things to *self*.

This is exactly what we see in America today. Hezekiah's response was to tear his clothes and cover himself with sackcloth. The tearing of clothes and the

---

[50] Isaiah 36:16

wearing of sackcloth is an expression of deep mourning and humility.

Hezekiah then says,

"This day is a day of distress, of rebuke, and of disgrace… therefore lift up your prayer for the remnant that is left." Isaiah 37:3–4

Hezekiah develops a true heart cry of repentance unto the Lord. He prays intently for the remnant of his day. Now, we too live in days of distress, rebuke, and disgrace. We must lift up our prayers for the remnant that is left. We must cry out to God like Hezekiah,

"So now, O Lord our God, save us, please, from his hand, that all the kingdoms of the earth may know that you, O Lord, are God alone" (Isaiah 37:20). Save us! Please! This must be our collective, repentant cry to the Lord! God responds to humble "sackcloth" prayers! To Hezekiah's prayer, his response was overwhelming:

"And that night the angel of the Lord went out and struck down 185,000 in the camp of the Assyrians. And when people arose early in the morning, behold, these were all dead bodies." Isaiah 37:36

God wants to send help to the earth, but he waits to be called upon because he gave man dominion over the earth. The victory awaits in humble prayer. The fight is not won with weapons of the flesh. The fight is won on our hands and knees. He awaits the heart cry of the remnant that seeks his face![3]

Daniel was another man who prayed for the remnant of his day. Daniel sought the Lord for 21 days in prayer and fasting for the remnant of Israel. The nation of Israel was returning to its homeland to build the second temple after the order of King Cyrus. On the twenty-first day of prayer and fasting an angel came to him and said,

"Fear not, Daniel, for from the first day that you set your heart to understand and humbled yourself before your God, your words have been heard, and I have come because of your words. The prince of the kingdom of Persia withstood me twenty-one days, but Michael, one of the chief princes, came to help me, for I was left there with the kings of Persia, and came to make you understand what is to happen to your people in the latter days. For the vision is for days yet to come." Daniel 10:12–14

---

[3] *Since the writing of this book, multiple states have pushed back against abortion. Some have even made it nearly impossible to get one. I believe this is an answer to prayer. Continue to intercede for our nation.*

From the first day that Daniel humbled himself his prayers were being heard in heaven. This is where the angel peels back the veil of this dimension and lets us see what really takes place in the spiritual realm. The angel was headed toward Daniel from day one but was held up in a battle with a fallen angel for twenty-one days! God responded to Daniels prayers and sent Michael the Archangel *(who is more powerful than Satan)* to help the unnamed Angel get through to Daniel so he was able to deliver the word to Daniel.

It was by persisting in prayer, humility and fasting that Daniel took part in this spiritual warfare. We must learn from this and take part ourselves,

"For the weapons of our warfare are not of the flesh but have divine power to destroy strongholds"[51]

---

[51] 2 Corinthians 4:5

"If we want revivals, we must revive our reverence for the Word of God. If we want conversions, we must put more of God's Word into our sermons; even if we paraphrase it into our own words, it must still be his Word upon which we place our reliance, for the only power which will bless men lies in that." -Spurgeon[52]

---

[52] The Complete Works of C. H. Spurgeon, Volume 38

CHAPTER THREE

Real Love

Jesus says, "Greater love has no one than this, that someone lay his life down for his friends" (John 15:13). Jesus not only laid his life down for us, he also calls us friend. What an honor it is to be a friend of God! Jesus ascended into heaven with holes in his hands, and for eternity he will wear our transgressions as scars on his body. "And if one asks him, 'What are these wounds on your back?' he will say, 'The wounds I received in the house of my friends'" (Zechariah 13:6). Words cannot contain the weight of this love that God has shown us.

    Jesus is perfect love. The Bible says that "God is love"[53]. Jesus himself is actually the embodiment of love. If Christ is perfect, undefiled love, then everything he says and does is in perfect love. Yet in Scripture we see Jesus constantly challenging people with really tough and often

---

[53] 1 John 4:8

offensive words and teachings. How can this be? How can God, being perfect love, make so many people feel uncomfortable and offended? It's because true love is often offensive. The love of Jesus can be so offensive that the Bible says it will even divide families.[54]

Growing up in a decaying society, we have been brainwashed to view any form of affirmation as love. It's the same concept that we see in youth sports now. Everyone gets a trophy. No one is allowed to hear the truth.

Society thinks we are helping people by giving them false affirmation when, in fact, it's the exact opposite. Only telling people things that make them feel good while avoiding the truth is actually very harmful and often insincere. Flattery and insincere praise are an abomination to the Lord. The book of Psalms actually says, "May the LORD cut off all flattering lips" (Psalm 12:3)! We should be very careful about what we say. We must think twice before telling our congregations to speak flattery to the person to their left and to their right.

*Rather, speaking **the truth in love**, we are to grow up in every way into him who is the head, into Christ,*

Ephesians 4:15

---

[54] Matthew 10:21–22

Much of this book is going to come off as offensive to a lot of people because true edification is aimed to help one grow, not get puffed up with conceit. I love you so much that I'd rather offend you with the truth than lie to you, pat you on the back, and see you end up in hell for eternity.

The word of God is offensive because our Father who wrote it through his Spirit loves us so much that he would only leave us with the honest truth and nothing else. God disciplines those that he loves. He knows what's best for us. We don't always want to hear the honest truth, because sometimes the truth hurts and makes us uncomfortable.

Don't live a lie. Don't be a slave to comfort, let the word of God help you to discern for yourself what true love is. A love that rejoices with the **TRUTH**:

*Love is patient, love is kind. It does not envy, it does not boast, it is not proud. It does not dishonor others, it is not self-seeking, it is not easily angered, it keeps no record of wrongs. Love does not delight in evil but rejoices with the **TRUTH**. It always protects, always trusts, always hopes, always perseveres. Love never fails.*[55]

---

[55] 1 Corinthians 13:4–8 (NIV)

Value

In Matthew 13:44-46, Jesus says "The kingdom of heaven is like treasure hidden in a field, which a man found and covered up. Then in his joy he goes and sells all that he has and buys that field." The treasure in the field represents the kingdom of God. Jesus is telling us that we can have the kingdom of God if we choose to trade in all that we have. This exchange was easy for the man in the parable. He recognized the kind of treasure he stumbled upon and valued it far above everything else he owned. The most important question in your brief vapor of a life is this, what do you value?

Most people look at the treasure in the field and simply don't find any value in it. They just step over it and continue on with their day. The Bible says, "For where your treasure is, there your heart will be also" (Matthew 6:21). If your treasure is in the kingdom of heaven, your heart will be there as well, and you will see clearly the value of the treasure in the field. If your treasure is in the world, your heart will be in the world. You won't see any value in the treasure in the field or be able to imagine why anyone would sell everything to buy it.

A gemologist only knows the value of stones by thoroughly studying them. The average person would step over priceless stones on the ground because they don't know what they're looking for. I recently saw a picture of a

1,758-carat diamond in the rough. This diamond was actually the second largest diamond in the world, and it is likely worth tens of millions of dollars. However, in its raw state it barely looked any different than a chunk of old charcoal from a fire pit. You would only know the value of this rock by studying rocks.

Similarly, in order to see value in the kingdom of God, you need to get down in the dirt, dust off the book and study Jesus. The more you get to know him, the more you will value him and the things of his kingdom.

My father collected baseball cards for a long time. He pretty much knows all there is to know about them. He'd tell you that people have used priceless baseball cards for book markers. One man's trash is another man's treasure. They dragged my treasure like trash through the streets of Jerusalem and hung him on a cross. What they treated like trash was the most valuable thing to ever touch the surface of the earth. This is why Jesus cried, "Forgive them, Father, for they have no idea what they're doing!"[56] That love right there is why I'm ready to give up anything to obtain Jesus. He is the treasure in the field.

As you grow in intimacy with the Lord, your values will start to shift from temporary to eternal things because you'll start to see where true value is. If you value Jesus more than the temporary pleasure of sin, you won't want to sin. If you don't value Jesus, you will see more value in sin

---

[56] (Luke 23:34, author's paraphrase).

and only keep away from sin as a form of religion or self-righteousness. John Piper said it perfectly, "Sin is what you do when your heart is not satisfied with God. No one sins out of duty. We sin because it holds out some promise of happiness. That promise enslaves us until we believe that God is more to be desired than life itself."[57]

Think about one of those old-fashioned scales. Now imagine Jesus sitting on one side and all the pleasures of the world sitting on the other. What weighs more to you? What do you place value on in life? Think heavily on this because what you value in this life will determine your eternity.

"By faith Moses, when he was grown up, refused to be called the son of Pharaoh's daughter, choosing rather to be mistreated with the people of God than to enjoy the fleeting pleasures of sin. He considered the reproach of Christ greater wealth than the treasures of Egypt, for he was looking to the reward." Hebrews 11:24–26

---

[57] John Piper, Future Grace: The Purifying Power of the Promises of God

Spirit & Truth

There's a theology that has plagued Christianity in America that worship is just the softening of the heart before the pastor preaches a sermon. That worship is just the music before the preacher teaches—two fast songs, one slow song to set the mood, and then we all sit down. We have somehow become concerned if the congregation enjoyed the worship as if it was for them. Meanwhile, the majority of the congregation isn't even participating but just looking around waiting for "worship" to be over so they can sit down. I believe this is what Scripture talks about when it says,

> "This people honor me with their lips, but their heart is far from me; in vain do they worship me, teaching as doctrines the commandments of men."[58]

Worship isn't just songs that we sing or something that we do; worship is supposed to be who we are. God's children are first worshipers above everything else in life. Your spiritual worship starts at the altar of sacrificed living, "present your bodies as a living sacrifice, holy and acceptable to God, which is your spiritual worship" (Romans 12:1). This is what sets the remnant apart. Many of the worship songs we sing aren't even about giving glory to God or expressing our love for him; they're about us and what God can do for us. I've seen Christians fall onto their

---

[58] Isaiah 29:13

knees, shout, jump, dance and cry over a football game on TV. Meanwhile, some of those same people look miserable while "worshipping" God earlier that same morning at church. Your actions will speak of who or what it is that you worship in life. Forget about how *your* worship experience was at church. We each have to ask ourselves, is *God* pleased with *my* worship? When you understand the reality of who is receiving your worship, your worship will become real. Worship is the overflow of love and adoration poured out from your heart to Gods. It is simply a response to who God is.

To truly worship the Lord in a manner pleasing to the Father, we must worship him in spirit and truth:

> "But the hour is coming, and is now here, when the true worshipers will worship the Father in spirit and truth, for the Father is seeking such people to worship him. God is spirit, and those who worship him must worship in spirit and truth."[59]

You can see the outward results of someone worshipping God in spirit, but you can't see worship done in spirit itself. Worship in spirit comes from the heart, mind and will of an individual that's choosing to align with heaven. Right now in heaven there are four living creatures around the throne of God whose entire bodies are covered in eyes just to gaze upon the glory of the Lord. Worship in spirit isn't focused on natural realities but entirely engaged in the spiritual

---

[59] John 4:23-24

realm where God dwells. Worship isn't about fancy lyrics or crafty musicians. There is only one song on repeat in heaven for all of eternity! "Holy, holy, holy, is the Lord God Almighty, who was and is and is to come!"[60]

The truth John is talking about is God's word. Jesus is referred to in the book of John as the *Word* and the *Truth*. We are to center our worship around Jesus and his works, the gospel. When spirit aligns with truth in worship something powerful happens. The atmosphere changes when God inhabits the praises of his people. God is raising up a generation who will worship him in spirit and truth, a remnant like David who long to gaze upon the beauty of the Lord all the days of their life.

Roadblocks

In the Christian world, we always throw around the terms "all in" and "sold out" or "on fire" to describe people who seem to be faithfully following Jesus. If we lived in the days of the first apostles, we wouldn't need these adjectives to describe a true follower of Jesus. Reason being, they would literally light Christians on fire (Roman candles) and place them all around the city of Rome. With this kind of

---

[60] Revelation 4:8

distinct message being displayed, you would think twice before calling yourself a Christian. Only the "on fire" Christians would be set on fire.

Fire is inevitable for everyone; you can't avoid it. You have to choose between the refining fire of God or the eternal lake of fire for those who reject God. The martyr was already on fire before being set on fire because he had the fire of the Holy Spirit upon him. The Holy Spirit's fire makes it possible to receive the martyr's fire with joy. There are several historic accounts of people being burned alive while worshiping the Lord. It's only by the power of the Holy Spirit that this is possible.

"Do not fear those who kill the body but cannot kill the soul. Rather fear him who can destroy both soul and body in hell." Matthew 10:28

I have three mentors from Nigeria. They have each left a distinct impact on my life. I admire their faith and their individual walks with the Lord. As I was communing with one of them a few months ago, our conversation left me with a heavy revelation.

Nigerian Christians have been under heavy attack from the Muslim Jihadist organization known as Boko Haram. Boko Haram has been creating roadblocks throughout the northern part of the country where they will stop your car in the middle of the road. If they come to the conclusion that you are a Christian, they will take you out into the bush and kill you. This has happened to hundreds of innocent Christians in Nigeria. As my brother was explaining this to me, I heard the Lord speak to me clearly, "American Christians have roadblocks that are killing them as well. But unlike your brothers and sisters in Nigeria whose roadblocks lead them to heaven, your roadblocks in America lead you to hell." I wept heavily after God spoke this to my heart.

What are your roadblocks? What is keeping you from living a life that is wholly devoted to the Lord? Is it drunkenness, unforgiveness, pride, lust, addiction, the love of money? The roadblocks Christians face in America might look a bit different from the roadblocks Christians face in northern Nigeria but the roadblocks in America are far deadlier. The overload of abundance in America has spoiled like fermented produce. The sour grapes have blurred the vision of many generations.

You must read the large street sign that is ahead of you. It says WARNING, DANGER AHEAD: "Do not let the comforts, pleasures and deceptions of sin divert you off the narrow path into the bush."

"Be sober-minded; be watchful. Your adversary the devil prowls around like a roaring lion, seeking someone to devour." 1 Peter 5:8

There have been more than one million Christian martyrs around the world in the last decade. Christians are persecuted in more than forty countries. I know this is hard to believe living in the American bubble—the media doesn't want you to know that Muslims kill Christians every single day around the world—but this is real.

I was in northern Nigeria this last summer. The day that I arrived at my destination close to seventy Christians were gunned down dead just a few hours away from where I was staying. A few days prior, five pastors were kidnapped, and to my knowledge their whereabouts are still unknown. This type of persecution is ongoing.

God might not be asking you to face the martyr's death, but he is requiring that your heart is willing to answer his call on your life no matter what or where he is calling you. We ask God in our prayers boldly but almost naively to make us like Jesus. Do we really understand what we are asking? Jesus was rejected by man, beaten beyond recognition and hung on a cross.

I want to pay respect to those who are laboring for the advancement of the gospel around the world and to those who have laid their lives down for the expansion of the gospel. Let us not forget our fallen soldiers, who are now truly more alive than ever in the presence of the Creator. It all started with twelve who knew Jesus intimately. We must get to know Jesus ourselves and carry out *The Great Commission*[61] without being distracted by numbers, platforms or budgets.

One by one the apostles gave their lives and considered it an honor to be martyred for Jesus. I pray we can all have the same heart and dedication to the Lord as the original forefathers of our faith in Christ Jesus;

Resting in His Presence

James son of Zebedee – Beheaded 44 AD

Andrew – Crucified sideways 60 AD

James son of Alpheus – Stoned 62 AD

Peter – Crucified upside down 64 AD

Jude – Crucified 65 AD

Paul – Beheaded 66 AD

Matthias – Burned alive * AD

Bartholomew – Skinned alive * AD

Thomas – Speared 72 AD

---

[61] "All authority in heaven and on earth has been given to me. [19] Go therefore and make disciples of all nations, baptizing them in the name of the Father and of the Son and of the Holy Spirit, [20] teaching them to observe all that I have commanded you. And behold, I am with you always, to the end of the age." (Matthew 28:16-20)

Simon the Zealot – Crucified 74 AD

Matthew – Stabbed 74 AD

Philip – Put to death* 80 AD

John – Boiled in oil 90 AD but wasn't harmed, exiled to death on Patmos.

"They gave our Master a crown of thorns, why do we hope for a crown of roses?" - Martin Luther

The Attack on Logic

Webster's 1828 definition and purpose of logic is:

>-The art of thinking and reasoning justly.

>-Logic is the art of using reason well in our inquiries after truth, and the communication of it to others.

>-The purpose of logic is to direct the intellectual powers in the investigation of truth, and in the communication of it to others.

Unfortunately, as of right now in the United States of America, you can legally pick your gender. You can even make a doctor cut your genitalia off and, in some cases, make taxpayer dollars pay for it. The even more unfortunate part is you'll have a group of supporters encouraging you, saying that you made the right decision. Logic will tell you that cutting your genitalia off is harmful and that if you have the desire to do so there is something wrong with that desire itself, not your genitalia. Logic will tell you that having either XY chromosomes or XX is sufficient for establishing your gender as male or female. Logic will tell you that men have specific DNA to create sperm to reproduce, and women have specific DNA, ovaries, and a womb to carry a living child for nine months and then give birth.

Logic went from being the pursuit of intellectual truth to the approval of emotional thinking and decisions. Emotions have always had the ability to overcome truth. That is why in the word, God stresses to us the importance of taking every thought or idea captive and having self-control. The vast majority of really bad decisions I've made, if not all of my really bad decisions were done out of emotional thinking and not true logical thinking. This goes for the rest of mankind as well. This is also why God tells us to be sober minded. God knows when we are not of sober mind, we tend to make more emotional based decisions and when your mind is not sober your emotions are all over the place. Much of our lives consists of battles between truth and emotions. Emotions can be our friends, but so often they are a wolf in sheep's clothing waiting to destroy us. God wants us to think logically in pursuit of truth. Satan wants us to be addicted and blinded to our emotions so we can't decipher what's right from wrong.

We must get back to true logical thinking in America. We cannot let an emotional, confused generation be our nations downfall.

True logic will tell you that a baby in the mother's womb moving around with a heartbeat is a human life. Yet over sixty million abortions have taken place on US soil. We all know about the tragic events of 9/11, but did you know that the same number of deaths that happened on 9/11 happen daily from abortion! As of right now it is legal in the state of New York to murder a baby in the womb up until the day of birth. None of this makes sense logically. Or even legally! If you were to crash your car into a pregnant woman and kill her and her baby (in womb), you would be charged with a *DOUBLE homicide*. Even if the woman was on her way to an abortion clinic to have the baby killed legally. The attack on logic doesn't seem to have any borders or boundaries.

Education in America was once logical in its pursuit of truth and knowledge. Harvard Universities seal and motto reads "VE-RI-TAS". The word veritas is Latin for *truth* and the truth is for over two hundred years Harvard's motto wasn't just *"Veritas"* it was *"Veritas Christo et Ecclesia"* ("Truth for Christ and the Church").

There's a therapy ban in several states, including Massachusetts, that doesn't legally allow you to tell your own child if they are a boy or a girl. Theoretically, If I had an eight-year-old boy who said, "Dad, I want to be a girl," the state government would consider it child abuse if I said,

"No, son, that's ridiculous." They could literally attempt to take my child from me. The same people who promoted this therapy ban are promoting child drag shows with half naked boys dressed as women in makeup. *THIS IS REAL!*

> *"But while his men were sleeping, his enemy came and sowed weeds among the wheat and went away."*
>
> Matthew 13:25

It is crucial that the remnant stays awake and stays aware of the enemy's tactics to confuse and manipulate the youth of America. It was while the church slept in America that the enemy came in and sowed his lies, deception and confusion. Do not be seduced into "political correctness". True political correctness is now truly nonexistent. This is a war for your mind and your children. *STAY AWAKE*, be bold and think logically.

Opium Drip

If someone is about to die at a hospital from a painful ailment or disease, doctors will hook that person up to an IV that has a continual, steady flow of painkillers. The person then stays in a sedated euphoric state of mind until they die. This is exactly what is happening to the entire nation of America outside of the hospital without anyone even knowing.

In 70AD Rome, Emperor Vespasian built the Colosseum. This massive structure could house 50,000 people at one time. This was unprecedented for that time period. The Colosseum was home to all sorts of gruesome events. The Roman elite would feed people to lions and even have gladiators fight each other to the death. This high level of entertainment was strategically designed to distract and pacify the city of Rome. To control and manipulate a large population, you need to keep them distracted and sedated. If you don't, the masses might try and figure out what's really going on in the world. There are now thousands of "Colosseums" around the United States full of millions of people on a weekly basis with millions more glued to their TV's watching these arenas from their couches. Sports are great, healthy and fun when they're not idolized. However, they're frequently idolized.

There has never been a more sedated civilization in the history of the world than today's America. Sports are just one of the many mind-numbing opium-like supplements that keep Americans sedated to the reality of their existence. In the chemical sense, doctors push mind-numbing drugs on millions of people every year. Social media has taken over as the main form of community which drives people into isolation. Video games and virtual reality have become a multibillion-dollar industry, to the point that neighborhoods once filled with kids playing now look abandoned. Families are abandoned for internet mistresses, romance novels and Hallmark movies. The majority of parents could care less what's really going on in their children's lives because they're far too focused on going out and drinking with their own friends. Maintaining a social life has become more important to many parents then their own children's well-being. I don't want to lose another generation to negligence! We have to snap out of this coma America!

America is beyond enslaved to instant gratification. "I want to feel good now!" is the heart cry of "Gen Z". Some of the designing programmers of Facebook openly admitted to creating social media to be addictive. Same with the software developers of Fortnite (a popular video game). Their goal was to make the most mentally addicting video game possible. Addiction is running rampant because people are searching for a way out of reality! This is right where the enemy wants you to be. Numb to reality! The only reason such ridiculous laws have been able to pass as of late, like the law that allows late-term abortion, is because the masses are so sedated by their own selfish interests, they have no reaction anymore:

"Did you know you can legally kill 9-month-old babies in New York now?"

"Oh, wow. That's crazy man…I wonder who's playing the Cowboys tomorrow."

Seriously, society has become so sedated that the masses only care about things that are directly related to their personal pleasure. Sadly, this same level of sedation has crept into the church. We've become so numb to religion and man's agenda we think goosebumps and good crowd energy are a move of the Holy Spirit!

I believe the majority of the American church has become numb and powerless because it is no less plugged into the world than those outside the church. Divorce and pornography addiction statistics are almost no different among people labeled "Christian" than among those not. Same with alcohol consumption and drug use.

It's time for *The Remnant* to unplug from the worlds sedatives and plug into the *Spirit of God*.

"How can you pull down strongholds of Satan if you don't even have the strength to turn off your TV?"

-Leonard Ravenhill

CHAPTER FOUR

Money

We've all heard the saying that money is the root of all evil. Well, that's not true. The scripture actually says it's the *love* of money that is the route of all evil, or all kinds of evil (1 Timothy 6:10). Some of you already knew that and have heard this same message preached before, but generally, this is where we stop. As long as you don't love money, then you're all set. We so often skip the verse before that says,

"those who desire to be rich fall into temptation, into a snare, into many senseless and harmful desires that plunge people into ruin and destruction." 1 Timothy 6:9

The desire to be rich is a snare that disguises itself as the "American Dream."

If we desire to be rich that desire itself *will* cause us to fall into temptation. The desire to be rich *will* entangle us. It *will* pull us into senseless and harmful desires that are contrary to the work of God. The desire to be rich will plunge us into ruin and destruction.

Most of us don't want to hear this. Generally, our way out of this scripture is to say to ourselves, "Well, I desire to be rich for the right reasons. If I'm rich I can give to whatever organization or person I want to freely and bless people with my money. I could even build a nice big church." This sounds good in theory. However, the warning isn't confined to any of your terms of agreements. The promise is that if you have the desire to be rich it *will* lead you astray from the Lord.

Matthew 6:24 is where we read, "No one can serve two masters, for either he will hate the one and love the other, or he will be devoted to the one and despise the other. You cannot serve God and money."

We are supposed to work hard and earn an honest living. There's nothing wrong with being rich. If God wants you to have wealth, you will have it for his glory and his good works. However, the *desire* itself is the deceiver.

If you desire to give generously to people and don't have a lot of money that's okay. We should desire to give like the apostles did:

"I have no silver and gold, but what I do have I give to you. In the name of Jesus Christ of Nazareth, rise up and walk!"
Acts 3:6

The desire to be rich comes with the desire for power. The rich man can point to a mountain and say "move" and it will move by the hands of the laborers he pays to move it. The reason God doesn't write every Christian a billion-dollar check is because he wants us to depend on him daily. Like I said before, dependency develops intimacy and God longs to be intimate with us. He knows we need him more than we know we need him. He made it impossible for his people to survive on yesterday's mana in the wilderness. He wants us to depend on him for fresh bread daily. When we acquire wealth, however, we can take things into our own hands without ever asking God.

When we truly desire Jesus above all else, everything changes. When Jesus gets involved, things get done that our wallets could never do no matter how full they are.

Two things I ask of you;

deny them not to me before I die: Remove far from me falsehood and lying; give me neither poverty nor riches; feed me with the food that is needful for me, lest I be full and deny you and say, "Who is the Lord?" or lest I be poor and steal and profane the name of my God.

Proverbs 30:7–9

Anointed vs. Peddler

Stop seeking your "calling" immediately. There is so much pressure these days to "find your calling." I see many new believers run off to seminary before they even read the Bible. Seek the *Giver* of your calling. His name is Jesus.

Many Christians see anointed people preach and say, "I want that anointing on my life." Anointing doesn't come over night. It comes from time spent in the secret place with Jesus. Anointing comes from spending so much intimate time with Jesus you drip the fragrance of his Spirit, his love, and his truth. There is a deep crushing process that has to happen in order to receive anointing. Anointing is never to be the desire; *Jesus is the sole desire.* Anointing is a by-product of being with Jesus and letting him crush you. Anointing doesn't come in your timing, but God's. Many people try to skip the crushing process, and as a result, they become peddlers of God's word:

> "But thanks be to God, who in Christ always leads us in triumphal procession, and through us spreads the fragrance of the knowledge of him everywhere. For we are the aroma of Christ to God among those who are being saved and among those who are perishing, to one a fragrance from death to death, to the other a fragrance from life to life. Who is sufficient for these things? For we are not, like so

many, peddlers of God's word, but as men of sincerity, as commissioned by God, in the sight of God we speak in Christ."[62]

The Anointed

The anointed one is in complete submission to the Lord. The anointed one is deeply in love with Jesus. The anointed one is commissioned by God, not man. The anointed one diffuses the fragrance of the Lord's knowledge wherever he is *led* to go by the Holy Spirit. The love of God emanates off of the anointed one, the aroma is so thick and heavy with truth it sometimes stings. Like saltwater in a wound, the sting always offers to bring healing to those who wish to receive it. The anointed one desires the secret place more than the stage. The anointed one overflows with fresh oil that leaves behind a trace wherever they go. The anointed one recognizes no one is sufficient to receive anointing but it's only by the grace of God, for the work and glory of God. The anointed one considers himself a sheep to be slaughtered. The anointed one has no agenda of their own. Love, joy, peace, patience, kindness, goodness, faithfulness, gentleness, and self-control are the fruits of their life.

---

[62] 2 Corinthians 2:14-17

The Peddler

The peddler goes where they see a need. The peddler pushes their agenda. The peddler is always branding their brand like a farmer on steer. The peddler believes they can control and instruct the Holy Spirit. The peddler replicates or mimics the anointed one. The peddler is adulterating the word of God, "pimping it out." The word Paul uses for "peddler" in Greek is *kapēleuō*. This is a word that would be used to describe a wine merchant who deceptively waters down their wine to sell it for a greater profit. The peddler desires to be rich. The peddler needs to be in control. The peddler sees the anointed as a threat. The peddler is convinced they are doing the work of God. The peddler feeds off of the praises, approval, and applause of man.

In biblical times, anointing was generally done with olive oil. In order to extract oil from an olive, there is an intense crushing process that has to happen. If you want the anointing of God on your life you have to let him crush you. You need to be crushed to the point that the person of "you" no longer exists, crushed to the point that all that is left in you is Jesus, who was crushed for you! When you're crushed by the Lord all of your desires and selfish ambitions get removed. Just like new wine flows from crushed grapes, the Holy Spirit flows through vessels fully submitted and crushed by the will of the Lord. You cannot bypass the crushing and receive anointing. You cannot bypass the crushing and receive new wine. Trust God. Trust his crushing process. Trust in *HIS* timing. He's making you into a vessel for honorable use.

When your life is hard-pressed for Christ, you will no longer look at the trials in life as a negative thing but as an opportunity for victory and growth.

> "For to me to live is Christ, and to die is gain. If I am to live in the flesh, that means fruitful labor for me. Yet which I shall choose I cannot tell. I am hard pressed between the two. My desire is to depart and be with Christ, for that is far better." Philippians 1:21–23

Paul was hard-pressed between fruitful labor and death. He considered death far better for the sake of unity with Christ, but for the sake of his disciples' progression in faith, he felt it was necessary to remain in his body. Are we hard-pressed like Paul? Are we hard-pressed between fruitful labor and death or between comfort and pleasure?

James, the half-brother of Jesus, was hard-pressed in his life. That is why he could boldly say,

> "Consider it pure joy, my brothers and sisters, whenever you face trials of many kinds, because you know that the testing of your

faith produces perseverance. Let perseverance finish its work so that you may be mature and complete, not lacking anything." James 1:2–4

All pressure in life is an opportunity to grow. Let the hard press of sanctification form you into the image of Christ. Just like Paul, may the remnant be found pressed between fruitful labor and death. Just like James, may the remnant be found joyful under trial, knowing that the pressing is producing oil and wine that will saturate the world.

Encounter

We are all somewhat familiar with the idea of "love languages" in marriage. This popular marriage advice says that there are five different "languages" that we use to express love: quality time, physical touch, gifts, words of affirmation, and acts of service. I'm sure you know right away the order in which you receive and give love. It's extremely important to be aware of these love languages when entering into marriage, but have you ever processed the fact that these love languages were designed and given to you by God? Yes, for your spouse, but even more so for your relationship with him!

Jesus is coming back as bridegroom for his *BRIDE*. The reason he designed you to receive and give love in these ways is because he himself receives and gives love in these ways. You were made for relationship. Our God is a relational, intimate being. If you belong to Christ, you are his bride! If you long to encounter the living God in a deeper way, start to reflect on the love languages he has instilled in you.

Relationships are a two-way street. It's our obligation to put forth effort in loving our spouse even when we don't feel like it. If our spouse receives love in a love language that we are not used to speaking, it's our obligation to learn it and speak it. It's no different in our walk with God. If we aren't expressing our love for God in all his known love languages, we are missing out on intimacy with him.

Unlike our human spouses, God is the perfect companion. He is without flaw. God has already given you more words of affirmation than any husband could ever come up with for his bride. Read the Song of Solomon! Have you ever told God how amazing he is? Do you sing songs of affirmation to him? You will touch his heart if you sing with a pure heart.

When you serve others in Jesus's name, the Bible says you are not only serving them, you're actually serving Jesus!

Quality time is one of God's deepest known love languages. However, it's often the most neglected by the busy American. God is jealous for you. He desires alone time with you without any distractions.

The physical touch of God is a real thing. If you haven't ever experienced his love in this way, ask for it! He longs to embrace you in his arms! Posture yourself in a way to receive the physical touch of God. His presence is tangible. Body language and body posture are ways of expressing physical love to the Lord. King David even danced unto the Lord! Getting on your hands and knees is not religious if your heart is postured correctly. Body posture reflects what is going on in your heart. Body posture is self-control. Your physical love moves God's heart!

The Father is the greatest giver of gifts. His gifts are endless. Even the struggles that produce fruit in us are a gift. The greatest gift of all is Christ Jesus our Lord and the free gift of salvation through his blood. It's in response to Christ's love that we give our lives as a gift back to God, fully submitted as a living sacrifice. When everything that we are and everything that we have belongs to God, you can be assured you have given properly.

The Holy Spirit comes into us as a response to our submission to Christ. He comes along with many supernatural gifts that glorify Jesus through our lives. The Spirit himself is a gift and it is essential to be filled and moved by him to have any true impact for the kingdom of heaven.

God never stops loving you for a second. He is the perfect lover. We are the ones who run from him, mess things up, and cause relationship issues. So, although the five love languages are important for you and your spouse, they are much more important for your relationship with God. For it is out of a healthy relationship with Jesus that all other relationships in your life are made right. There are thousands of *Christian marriage* books in the world. Though many of those books have great advice, I believe there is truly only one sentence necessary for a healthy, happy, prosperous marriage.

> *If both husband and wife are passionately and actively in love with Jesus on a daily basis, their marriage will flourish as the Holy Spirit makes habitation in their bodies and in their home.*

Cover Me

I heard the great evangelist Daniel Kolenda once say, "The armor of God in Ephesians chapter six doesn't have any armor for the back of your body because your brother is supposed to have your back in battle."

If that's how God made his army to operate, why are we competing with one another in ministry? Unfortunately, this isn't anything new. Roughly two thousand years ago, there were men who were happy that the apostle Paul was imprisoned so they could gain Paul's followers. Even though these preachers' motives were corrupt, Paul rejoiced that the gospel of Jesus Christ was being preached.[63]

Long before Paul, Korah and his followers accused Moses of poor leadership and tried to overthrow him and God's anointed. I see this same deceptive heart throughout Christianity today. It shouldn't matter what Christian brand or logo you associate with. If you are truly a brother or sister in Christ, I should go to war for you, not against you.

I want my brothers and sisters to have my back in battle, not waging war against me. It's sadly a rare thing nowadays to find a brother in Christ who is totally for you with no ulterior motive. It seems as if everyone's plundering the internet to make their own name famous. The many platforms of social media are mostly used for competition now, although they were originally designed to bring people together. There's only one name we should be striving *together* to make famous, the name of Jesus!

The apostle Paul had this same struggle in sending Timothy to Philippi. "I hope in the Lord Jesus to send Timothy to you soon, so that I too may be cheered by news of you. For I have no one like him, who will be genuinely concerned for your welfare" (Philippians 2:19–20). At one point even the apostle Paul had no one close to him but Timothy who would actually be concerned about the true welfare of others. The depravity of the human heart is far worse than we'd like to admit.

---

[63] Philippians 1:18

People are like onions. Yes, the vegetable. Once you start pealing back the layers of *"why we do what we do"*, you'll start to notice *self* is revealed more and more the deeper you go. It's for this reason that "He must increase, but I must decrease" (John 3:30).

The last days remnant needs to be a nameless generation that throws out the old wineskin—the old wineskin of "my platform," "my movement," "my church," "my ministry," "my conference," "my stage," "my agenda," "my vision," "my microphone," "my glory."

The remnant has many differences. Think about all the different branches, positions and professions in the US military. Imagine if the Army called the Navy in for backup during war and the Navy said, "no thanks, good luck though." This would NEVER happen! Each branch of the military is very different but all equally important. At the end of the day, they all have each other's back in battle because they all take commands from the same Commander in Chief. Similarly, the remnant takes their commands from the same Commander of the Lord's Army[64], Jesus.

A kingdom divided cannot stand. If the enemy's military can figure this out, the remnant sure has to. The enemy is severely outnumbered and overpowered! But he has Christians fooled into thinking he's not because he has us fighting each other instead of him! As the day of

---

[64] Joshua 5

Christ's return approaches, unity must grow stronger in the body of Christ! He desires us to be one! The world should know us by our love for one another![65]

> *"For the weapons of our warfare are not of the flesh but have divine power to destroy strongholds. We destroy arguments and every lofty opinion raised against the knowledge of God, and take every thought captive to obey Christ."*[66]

Not So Fast

It seems like every other week there's another health and fitness craze that comes to the forefront of society. As of late, several variations of fasting have been catching on. Intermittent fasting is becoming one of the favorite "get healthy" methods of mainstream nutritionists, personal trainers, and dietitians. Fasting has been proven to provide your body with all sorts of health benefits when done properly. This is of no surprise to the remnant because God has been telling us to fast for thousands of years and he wouldn't tell us to do something that would be harmful for us. The real health benefits of fasting, however, are related to the health of your spirit. If done properly, fasting will

---

[65] John 13:35
[66] 2 Corinthians 10:4–5

help you draw closer to God and you'll become more aware of your need for him.

The whole point of fasting is to deny the flesh what it hungers for so you can feast on bread from heaven (Jesus). There's an old Native American saying about two different wolves: "The one you feed is the one you see." It's the same with your flesh and your spirit. Jesus told us clearly that he himself is living water and the bread of life. We need to feed on him daily to stay alive spiritually.

The purpose of communion reflects the heart of this same concept. The point Jesus was making in communion is that you need to feed on him to stay alive. Christ Jesus is the Word, and his Word is him[67]. When you spend time with the Word, you are feeding your spirit. This is why the disciples couldn't fast when they were with Jesus. There was no need to fast when they stood face to face with the bread of heaven. Now that Jesus has ascended into heaven, fasting helps close gap.

The idea of fasting is intimidating to some people. Many Christians have never even thought about actually fasting. However, Jesus doesn't ask *if* you fast, he says *when* you fast (Matthew 6:16). It is implied by Jesus that fasting is part of your life as a Christian and should become common practice of all Christians. The word *fast* in Hebrew actually means to cover your mouth. You're not actually fasting by turning off your social media. These

---

[67] John 1:14

types of "fasts" are a clear example of what happens when culture influences faith. However, practicing any level of self-control is important. "Feeding the flesh" isn't just eating food. Food is just the tip of the iceberg. Anything that your body tells you that it needs or wants, making you respond to its commands becomes "feeding the flesh". Of course, we need some things that are healthy to survive—warm shelter, water, food—but the less we have controlling us the better. This is why I encourage people to stay away from addictive substances all together. The fact that most coffee drinkers can't physically function without coffee shows you how heavy the dependency can become. This isn't meant to condemn anyone, some of my heroes in the faith were avid cigar smokers. (Granted there was ignorance in their time period of what was healthy and what was not.)

It's just interesting how we Christians judge the guy at the front door of the church building smoking a cigarette and pass by him blocking our noses while holding a large double espresso mochaccino. There really aren't many differences chemically between caffeine and nicotine. They're both stimulants. You're an addict just like the guy smoking a cigarette. So, think twice about judging him next time. Even sugar is now being exposed as an addictive substance. Sugar can be just as deadly as tobacco! It's all relative, and my intention isn't to point anyone out in particular. The point is to hopefully realize how easily we can become enslaved to the fleshes demands. Where do we run to for comfort and satisfaction of the soul? If it's to anything or anyone but Jesus, our priorities are off.

Fasting is a weapon for spiritual breakthrough, but for some reason it has become "old-fashioned" in a lot of circles. Same goes for addressing the sin of gluttony. Self-control is learned through practice. The self-discipline of fasting is an incredible blessing that we need to take hold of.

The United States was once a great nation of prayer and fasting. Many US presidents even held national days of prayer and fasting. History shows us time and time again that before any great move of God there comes a wave of great prayer and fasting.

The prophet Ezra returned his people to the land of Israel. Such a great venture required a great fast. Ezra recounts,

"Then I proclaimed a fast there, at the river Ahava, that we might humble ourselves before our God, to seek from him a safe journey for ourselves, our children, and all our goods...."The hand of our God is for good on all who seek him, and the power of his wrath is against all who forsake him." So we fasted and implored our God for this, and he listened to our entreaty."[68]

Who does God listen to?

Those who humble themselves, fast, and seek his face.

---

[68] Ezra 8:21-23

Fasting comes down to the heart, not the act itself. Fasting serves no spiritual purpose if it's just a religious practice or a means of getting "six-pack abs". In those cases, the act of fasting will actually be counterproductive and pull you further away from God. So, make sure if you are going to fast, you're going into it with the right motivation.[69]

God isn't impressed with your ability to starve yourself. Angels moved at the prophet Daniels words, not his 3-week vegetable diet. It's faith that moves mountains, not fasting. However, fasting will increase your faith as you see Jesus clearer when you're fasting.

We fast because we desperately need Jesus!

We Christians love using this prophetic revival scripture in Joel,

"And it shall come to pass afterward, that I will pour out my Spirit on all flesh; your sons and your daughters shall prophesy, your old men shall dream dreams, and your young men shall see visions."[70]

This prophetic word is amazing! I believe such an outpouring of the Spirit is coming soon to America, but we seem to neglect the fact that the Lord calls us to repent and *fast* twice in the same chapter before this! This outpouring of the Holy Spirit in Joel chapter two is the result of true

---

[69] Read Isaiah chapter 58.
[70] Joel 2:28

repentance, humility, fasting and prayer!

"Yet even now," declares the Lord, "return to me with all your heart, with fasting, with weeping, and with mourning;

Blow the trumpet in Zion; consecrate a fast; call a solemn assembly" [71]

The Lord is looking for us to rend our hearts, not our garments. The American Church is far too pompous to see revival take place right now. Our pride an arrogance gives off a stench that reaches heavens gates. Until Gods people become humble, broken vessels, we will not see the outpouring of his Spirit over America.

Revival will not come to America until the church takes part in prayer, humiliation and fasting. Lord God bring healing to our land!

---

[71] Joel 2:12,15

Latter Rain

"then I will give you the rain for your land in its season, the early rain and the latter rain, that you may gather in your grain, your new wine, and your oil."

The prophet Moses declared that there would be two rains before harvest. An early rain and a latter rain. Moses wasn't alone in this prophecy, but the prophets Joel, Hosea and Zechariah chimed in on these two rains as well. The harvest would not come until both rains had fallen and produced a crop that was ripe for harvest.

The rain they prophesied about is the outpouring of the Holy Spirit and the harvest they are referring to is the harvest of the Lords people. The world felt the first rain two thousand years ago at Pentecost. Peter even referenced the prophet Joel after the first rain came upon them.

I believe the world is feeling the latter rains today. I believe we are currently living in the season of latter rain. Although America is lacking in comparison, the world is seeing unprecedented revival and outpouring of the Holy Spirit. The first season of rain started as a single cloud over the upper room and traveled throughout the world.

I believe the latter rain is currently making its way around the earth seeking seeds that are in good soil and those whose hearts are wholly devoted to the Lord.

We must pray that the latter rains make their way to America! I believe there are pop up storms in America happening already, but we need to ask God for a flood!

"Ask the LORD for rain In the time of the latter rain. The LORD will make flashing clouds; He will give them showers of rain, Grass in the field for everyone." [72]

I believe we are living in the days of latter rain where the clouds of Gods glory are traveling the globe making grass for everyone! These pop up thunderstorms of latter rain will fall on any people who ask for rain with pure hearts, hearts that are wholly devoted to the Lord!

The Lord isn't coming back for empty fields! He's coming back for a mighty harvest! We must ask for one last outpouring of the Holy Spirit in America. A rain so heavy that all of the walls man built around Jesus would wash away! A rain so heavy that the fields of America would burst with fresh crops!

Ask for rain! The harvest is near!

"And it shall come to pass afterward, that I will pour out my Spirit on all flesh; your sons and your daughters shall prophesy, your old men shall dream dreams, and your young men shall see visions. Even on the male and female servants in those days I will pour out my Spirit. "And I will show wonders in the heavens and on the earth, blood and

---

[72] Zechariah 10:1 (NKJV)

fire and columns of smoke. ***The sun shall be turned to darkness***, and the moon to blood, before the great and awesome day of the Lord comes."[73]

---

[73] Joel 2:28-31

CHAPTER FIVE

Come Out of Her

My father grew up in the Catholic Church, people have told me my entire life that there are many people within the Catholic Church that deeply love Jesus. I believe that to be true, the remnant is scattered far and wide. So, please listen to me clearly. Do not confuse my words! I am not judging the individuals inside the Catholic Church. There have been many people throughout history that have been used mightily by God from within the Catholic Church. The Catholic Church uses biblical scripture, that itself opens up the opportunity for anyone within to hear it, repent and make Christ Jesus their Lord.

    Just over 500 years ago, Martin Luther exposed ninety-five heretic practices of the Roman Catholic Church, and he almost lost his life because of it. All these years later I believe it is absolutely necessary to once again publicly shine light on the darkness of the Catholic Church.

There are hundreds of denominations of Christianity. I've been to many different churches in the States and several around the world. There are fruitful churches of all sorts of denominations. There are also unfruitful churches of the same denominations. There is no perfect denomination! Some churches are more biblically accurate than others. No denomination, church or Christian ever gets 100% on the scale of biblical accuracy.

We have to be very careful about how we go about exposing false doctrine and false prophets. This can be extremely shaky ground that many jump on to and quickly become the accuser of the brethren. I don't take any of this lightly.

However, what I can say with certainty and a clear conscious before the Lord is that at its **core**, Roman Catholicism is heretic, and if you believe in Jesus and you are a Catholic, you should come out of her immediately.

Roman Catholicism is the false face of Christianity to the entire world. It has been for centuries. Their doctrine has plagued New England for over two hundred years. I believe the great deceiver's greatest masterpiece has been the Roman Catholic Church itself.

I will tell you with certainty and sincerity, that the Catholic Church has immensely false doctrine and we should not strive for unity with the Catholic Church itself. If we only just look through history, we see a clear streak of heresy all throughout the life of the Catholic Church.

The pope himself accepting the title of "holy father"[74] is just the tip of the iceberg. Throughout every century of Catholicism, we can pull out heretic statements from Popes like:

"I alone am the successor of the apostles, the vicar of Jesus Christ, I alone have the mission to guide and direct the barque of Peter, I am the way, the truth, and the life.[1]"

"The Pope and God are the same, so he has all power in Heaven and earth.[2]"

"We hold upon this earth the place of God Almighty.[3]"

"The Pope is not simply the representative of Jesus Christ. On the contrary, he is Jesus Christ Himself, under the veil

---

[74] Matthew 23:9
[1] Pope Pius IX, quoted in Henry Charles Sheldon, *History of the Christian Church* (Peabody: Hendrickson Publishers, 1988), 59.
[2] Pope Pius V quoted in William Barclay, *Of the avthoritie of the pope : whether and how farre forth, he hath power and authoritie ouer temporall kings and princes : liber posthumus* (London: Arnold Hatfield, 1611), 218.
[3] Pope Leo XIII, *The Reunion of Christendom*, encyclical letter, Papal Encyclicals Online, June 20, 1894, https://www.papalencyclicals.net/leo13/l13praec.htm.

of the flesh. Does the Pope speak? It is Jesus Christ who is speaking, hence, when anyone speaks of the Pope, it is not necessary to examine but to obey.4"

I'm going to use the Catholic Church's **current doctrine** to reveal how unbiblical and heretic their doctrine is. The CCC (the Catechism of the Catholic Church) is the main source of Catholic doctrine. It is easily accessible on the internet or at a library. The Catholic Church teaches that the CCC is *equal* to the word of God. Those aren't my words but theirs. The CCC says that the Catholic Church has the inability to fail because the pope carries the authority of Christ. If the Pope gets "divine revelation," the Catholic Church then teaches the pope's revelation as equal to God's word. I'm serious. Read it for yourself:

"The supreme degree of participation in the authority of Christ is ensured by the charism of infallibility. This infallibility extends as far as does the deposit of divine Revelation; it also extends to all those elements of doctrine, including morals, without which the saving truths of the faith cannot be preserved, explained, or observed.5"

---

4 Pope Pius X, *Evangelical Christendom*, (London: J.S. Phillips, 1895), 49:15.
5 *Catechism of the Catholic Church*, 2nd ed., 2035.

"Both Scripture and Tradition must be accepted and honored with equal sentiments of devotion and reverence.[6]"

This is literally saying that any Catholic tradition is *EQUAL* to the Word of God.

"The task of interpreting the Word of God authentically has been entrusted solely to the Magisterium of the Church, that is, to the Pope and to the bishops in communion with him.[7]"

This states that *only* the Catholic Church has the authority to interpret Scripture.

"Moved by the Holy Spirit, we can merit for ourselves and for others all the graces needed to attain eternal life, as well as necessary temporal goods.[9]"

This literally says that grace and salvation can be earned. Not through faith like the Bible says but literally earned.

---

[6] *Catechism of the Catholic Church*, 2nd ed., 82.
[7] *Catechism of the Catholic Church*, 2nd ed., 100.
[9] *Catechism of the Catholic Church*, 2nd ed., 2027.

The bible tells us that God's grace is received by faith *ALONE*. (Ephesians 2:8-9)

"Therefore, the Blessed Virgin is invoked in the Church under the titles of Advocate, Helper, Benefactress, and Mediatrix.[10]"

This isn't referring to the Holy Spirit or Jesus. It's talking about Mary, the mother of Jesus. It is taught as doctrine equal to the Word of God in the Catholic Church that Mary is your advocate, mediator, and helper. When the Bible clearly states,

"For there is one God, and there is one **mediator** between God and men, the man Christ Jesus." (1 Timothy 2:5)

"My little children, I am writing these things to you so that you may not sin and if anyone sins, we have an **Advocate** with the Father, Jesus Christ the righteous." (1 John 2:1)

"But the **Helper**, the Holy Spirit, whom the Father will send in My name, He will teach you all things, and bring to

---

[10] *Catechism of the Catholic Church*, 2nd ed., 969.

your remembrance all that I said to you." (John 14:26)

Your Mediator and your Advocate is Jesus Christ alone. Your Helper is his Spirit. Mary was a sinner just like you and me, as "all have sinned and fall short of the glory of God" (Romans 3:23).

"Taken up to heaven she did not lay aside this saving office but by her manifold intercession continues to bring us the gifts of eternal salvation.[11]"

There is no biblical account for any of this. Mary does not intercede for us or give us salvation! Jesus does:

"Consequently, he is able to save to the uttermost those who draw near to God through him, since he always lives to make intercession for them." (Hebrews 7:25)

Next we see:

"By asking Mary to pray for us, we acknowledge ourselves

---
[11] Ibid.

to be poor sinners and we address ourselves to the 'Mother of Mercy,' the All-Holy One. We give ourselves over to her now, in the Today of our lives.[12]"

Asking Mary for *anything* is praying to Mary, which is an abomination! "If you give yourself over to Mary you are giving yourself over to Satan, not Mary!

The Catholic Church worships their own version of Mary, a false idol. The Catholic Church is chock full of idol worship. They have been for centuries. Much of which is in the form of prayer to the saints. The Catholic Church teaches that Mary herself was sinless. Pope Francis said, "Without Mary there would be no Jesus."[13] You're wrong, sir. Jesus made Mary. Jesus created the world:

"For by him all things were created, in heaven and on earth, visible and invisible, whether thrones or dominions or rulers or authorities—all things were created through him and for him." (Colossians 1:16)

---

[12] *Catechism of the Catholic Church*, 2nd ed., 2677.
[13] "Pope at Santa Marta: Learning from Our Lady of Sorrows," *Vatican Radio*, September 15, 2014, http://www.archivioradiovaticana.va/storico/2014/09/15/pope_at_santa_marta_learning_from_our_lady_of_sorrows/en-1106542.

Jesus is the Creator coming into his own creation. Jesus is no less God than his Spirit and the Father are God. If you miss that, you miss the gospel entirely.

When a Popes words are received as Gods word you've allowed over 200 men to add and take away from the actual word of God. The Catholic Church also adds seven historical books to their Bible. Books that the ancient Jews, Jesus himself and the apostles did not consider inspired by God. The result of this mass collection of "doctrine" is a false face of Christianity that has led millions astray from the heart of God and down a long road of heretic religion.

I don't believe people generally have malicious intent when saying that the Christian should unite with the Catholic Church. I don't think people have fully understood the level of heresy and corruption within Catholic Church history or even their current doctrine.

There have been multiple attempts of reformation within the Catholic Church throughout history that got shutdown quickly. In 1978 *Pope John Paul I* was going to bring major changes to the Catholic faith, he was allegedly assassinated 33 days after his inauguration. During the late 1970's Vatican Bank scandal, multiple people were allegedly assassinated. A Vatican banker who was closely affiliated with the elite Freemasons of Italy was found dead hanging from a bridge. I met with a man whose father knew this banker personally. His father was a journalist that was closely following this scandal in Europe and suspiciously died before ever getting his full story out. In 2012 Pope Benedict XVI commissioned a top-secret investigation into the Vatican Bank. This investigation was documented in a 300-page binder by three of the Popes top men. Not only was financial corruption brought to light, but also many forms of immoral behavior such as men in the Vatican hierarchy dressed in drag performing sexual acts with male prostitutes. The darkness of the Vatican cannot be ignored any longer. I know far too many people that have been molested in the greater Boston area alone by Catholic priests. The spirit of the Antichrist rests heavily within the Catholic Church.

Between 1960 and 1990 over **300,000** babies were kidnapped after birth and sold by the Catholic Church in Spain. Three hundred thousand! The mothers were told that their child had died overnight in the hospital, when in reality they were simply removed from the hospital. Similar criminal investigations continue worldwide. 16,000 babies were forced into adoption around the same time period in the U.K. These babies were born to unmarried mothers, so the Catholic Church took matters into their own hands and had their way with the children.

The Catholic Church does not allow anyone in the position of Pope to have a wife. Which is extremely odd for multiple biblical reasons, but none more peculiar than the fact that the Catholic Church firmly claims that the apostle Peter was their first Pope.

Peter had a wife...[75]

There is a very large and growing number of openly homosexual Catholic priests around the world. There are many Catholic churches around the world that even celebrate homosexuality. This is a great concern for the future of Christianity.

In his recent book *In the Closet of the Vatican* French journalist Frédéric Martel conducted 1,500 interviews with Vatican priests, guards, bishops, cardinals, ambassadors, diplomatic officials and other Vatican elites. His grand census after this deep and intense study was that roughly 80 percent of the Roman Catholic clergy that works directly around the Pope are homosexual.[76]

There is a major shift coming to the world and we have to be ready for it. It is only a matter of time before the Catholic Church publicly accepts homosexuality worldwide. They already do in many closed circuits.

Saying that the Christian church should unite with

---

[75] Matthew 8:14
[76] https://www.thetablet.co.uk/news/11356/explosive-new-book-lifts-lid-on-gay-priests-in-the-vatican
12 FEBRUARY 2019, THE TABLET Explosive new book lifts lid on gay priests in the Vatican by Christopher Lamb

the Catholic Church is equally heretic as saying the Christian church should unite with Mormons or the Jehovah's Witnesses. All three teach from the Bible a false manipulated doctrine made up of man and influenced by the great deceiver. All three add their own twisted doctrine to the true word of God.

Anyone can fabricate their own version of Jesus if they want to. We need to be able to discern the truth about who it is we serve. That's why intimacy is so important. Knowing Jesus personally and knowing his word is everything.

Just recently, Pope Francis and Sheik el-Tayeb, one of the leading authoritative figures for Sunni Muslims around the world, signed "A Document on Human Fraternity for World Peace and Living Together." The globalist agenda is moving faster than anyone could imagine. With the Pope having the ability to speak "divine revelation," anything could happen at any time.

All roads lead to Rome. Biblical prophecy is coming to fruition about the reformation of the Roman Empire. The merging peace between Islam, Catholicism, and Judaism is setting the stage for the Antichrist, who could charm them all in one accord. The enemy's throne is being built. The most deceptive days in the history of the world are here.

The Bible warns us in these last days, "false Christ's and false prophets will arise and perform great signs and wonders, so as to lead astray, if possible, even the elect."[77]

When religions unite to pray to one god, be assured it is not the God of the Bible that they are praying to.

Romanism

After the ascension of Jesus, his disciples spread the gospel throughout the Middle East, Asia and even into the heart of Rome. Empowered by the Spirit of God there was no stopping the advancement of *The Way*. Thousands upon thousands of people were being baptized in the name of the Father, the Son and the Holy Spirit. The most unlikely of conversions were taking place, including that of Roman soldiers. The name, the fame, and the power of Jesus was quickly spread throughout the earth.

There is no "proper" gathering size or specific location for the church to gather. What we know for sure is that we are not to forsake the gathering of the body.[78] God designed the church for community and fellowship in him. As of recently many Christians have debated what the biblical model of church actually looks like. We can

---

[77] Matthew 24:24
[78] Hebrews 10:25

quickly get religious in this aspect and try to fit every church body into a specific mold. I don't believe the size or location has ever really mattered to God. I think it's clear in his word that he is mainly concerned about the heart condition and direction of the body. A pure heart posture of the gathering is far more important than the amount of people or the location of the gathering.

The unity that is coming to the body of Christ in these last days must center on Jesus. A true Jesus people is arising. If our collective focus is to pour out our love and affection on him, it shouldn't matter what church we come from.

There is temptation here for some to shy away from the structure, accountability and discipline that comes along with belonging to a local church. There are many important, biblical guidelines for the body of Christ, so we have to be careful about abandoning structure all together in the pursuit of "freedom" in Christ.

However, until about 300AD the early church mainly gathered in what we'd call house churches today. The communion table was always at the center of their gatherings and partaking of the Lord together was a key element of the church's unity and fellowship in the presence of God. I believe Jesus was serious about communion when he said "Do this as often as you drink it"[79] I believe reflecting, remembering, discerning and

---

[79] 1 Corinthians 11:25

declaring the Lord Jesus while gathering as the church is essential and lacking in modern-day Christianity. Communion has become taboo in many evangelical Christian circles. I'm not going to say that the grape juice and bread turn into the actual red blood cells and tissue of Jesus in your mouth. What I am saying is that when you gather in his name and discern his body properly during communion, your spirit man ingest the real body and blood of Jesus and I know for a fact that this has physical ramifications. When people didn't properly discern the body Paul even said, "That is why many of you are weak and ill, and some have died."[80] Jesus is with us always, but the presence of the Lord is in union with his communion. With his presence comes healing and the fullness of life. This way of reverently communing around, in and through Jesus needs return to the body of Christ in America.

For roughly 300 years after Jesus ascended, Christianity flourished in the face of the most inhumane persecution from the Roman Empire. *The Way* flourished so much that many Roman citizens even became Christians during these years. Some of them met in literal underground churches.

As Christian customs slowly became more "Roman" in fashion, the persecution of Christians in Rome slowed down. I believe this was a direct result of watered down and diluted theology. True Christianity comes with a

---

[80] 1 Corinthians 11:30

promise of persecution and a blessing along with it.[81]

The doctrine of demons will settle on anything that distracts the masses from *The Way* himself. The apostle Paul prophesied about this in his first letter to Timothy.[82]

"Now the Spirit expressly says that in later times some will depart from the faith by devoting themselves to deceitful spirits and teachings of demons, through the insincerity of liars whose consciences are seared, who forbid marriage and require abstinence from foods that God created to be received with thanksgiving by those who believe and know the truth."[83]

In roughly 300AD a power struggle broke out in Rome, the future Emperor "Constantine the Great" had a supernatural encounter with the sun. Oddly enough, one day while preparing for battle, Constantine (who was a faithful Pagan) saw a cross appear in the middle of the sun and simultaneously heard a voice that said, "you are to concur in this sign." He did so and would eventually take over both the Western & Eastern Roman Empire.

---

[81] Matthew 5:10-12 & 2 Timothy 3:12
[82] The Catholic Church would go on to forbid marriage within leadership and forbid the eating of meat on Fridays.

[83] 1 Timothy 4:1-3

As Emperor, Constantine would officially change the faith of the entire Roman Empire to Christianity. This might sound good at first. Many Christians have taught and believed it was God that he encountered in the sun. I think very differently.

Constantine went on to change the Sabbath to Sunday in honor of the Pagan "sun god" Apollo. He even went as far as putting Apollo on Roman currency. This was the beginning of a long road of heresy known as the Roman Catholic Church.

The Roman Empire would eventually turn statues of Pagan Gods into statues of the saints. Constantine lived a very paganized form of Christianity and it is still unknown for sure if he ever really denounced Paganism entirely.

Although there have been many attempts in the past from Christians to separate themselves from the Romanized way of doing Christianity, I'm not sure as many groups were as successful as they thought, even the Separatist Pilgrims. What I mean by this is that the Romanization of *The Way* hasn't been entirely abandoned by even some of the most "separated" of denominations.

Earlier we talked about *The Way* being the original blueprint lifestyle that Jesus left the apostles to walk in as they gathered and lived as the ecclesia (church). The Roman Catholic Church consumed *The Way* by brute force very early on. In doing so the Romans built the foundation of the Catholic Church over the foundation of the remnant church. This was a clear tactic of Satan to hide the narrow path in a maze of religion.

Many people are not going to like that I'm saying this, but most evangelical churches are still built off of the Roman model of doing church opposed to *The Ways* model of being the church. What America needs in these last days is not another reformation. What America desperately needs is restoration to *The Way,* his name is Jesus. This is a call to shut down your 501C3's if they're not rooted in *The Way* himself. The days of institutionalized, Romanized religion have to end so *The Way* can take preeminence once again.

The beautiful thing is that *The Way* can never truly be manipulated or destroyed because *The Way* is not of this world.

The Romanization of Christianity was a tactic of the enemy to slow down the advancement of *The Way*. This was done by limiting the awareness and power of the Spirit by watering down and manipulating the truth. When Christianity is institutionalized, and everybody is a "Christian" it's a lot harder to actually reach people for Christ. Just ask anyone that evangelizes in Dallas, Texas. You can have the bible memorized in 3 languages and still not know *The Way*.

There's an old saying "if you can't beat them, join them". If you can recall the girl that followed the apostle Paul around everywhere shouting "These men are servants of the Most High God, who proclaim to you the way of salvation."[84] This sounds good on paper but she was in fact demonized and Paul casted that disruptive and distracting spirit right out of her. The *great deceiver* is very smart and wants nothing more than to cast disruption, delusion and confusion around the true gospel message. This is exactly what we see throughout history in the Catholic Church and its exactly what we see in the Christian Church of America today.

We mustn't forget that Satan has the power to give authoritative positions to whomever he wants on earth.[85] God is of course the supreme authority that has a hook in the mouth of every nation, but God uses the devil to work out a greater plan for mankind. There's no rivalry between God and that wicked serpent. God owns all things even the devil. He plans to use and dispose of Satan like an old dirty mop. That old dirty mop serves some purpose for now.

From the life of Constantine on, we see roughly 1200 years of absolute chaos in the world surrounding the Roman Church. I'm not going to go too in depth but if you wish to, please consider John Dowling's *The History of Romanism 1871 edition*.

I will say, I believe the biggest problem within these 1200 years was that unless you were super wealthy or extremely powerful it was very unlikely for you to get your

---

[84] Acts 16:17
[85] Luke 4:6

hands on a Bible. So, political and religious leaders used the word of God for power and control. I'm not saying that there weren't pockets of the remnant along the way within or around the Catholic Church. There absolutely were. In 726AD Emperor Leo blamed Catholic idol worship as the reason his empire was falling against the Islamic regime.[86] However, Emperor Leos attempt to remove all Catholic idols unfortunately failed after Pope Gregory viscously put up a fight to keep all graven images intact.

The message I'm trying to convey is that *The Way* himself is for the poor in spirit, not the high and lofty. Unfortunately, for 1200 years it was predominantly the high and lofty that had control of the word of God. Again, I can't discredit the gospel moving around the world during these years. God often uses imperfect people to do his will. However, most of the remnant's history is not clearly seen in the history books through these years.

From 300AD to 1500AD there were many great empires that rose to power and fell in the world. During this time period there were many off shoots of Catholicism and Orthodox Christianity that also spread throughout the world. However, Roman Catholicism continued to find its way to the top of the religious totem pole. They often did this by brute force. Even today nearly half of all Christians in the world identify as Roman Catholic.

---

[86] The History of Romanism v. iii Pg. 199
* Islam rose out of the desert in 610 AD and became a world powerhouse. Muhamad encountered an angel of light named Satan.

In the dawn of the 16th century *EVERYTHING* would begin to change. The word of God was translated into multiple languages and eventually dispersed to the masses. The Bible finally got into the hands of *the poor in spirit* and the world has never been the same!

God created the world out of nothing, and so long as we are nothing, He can make something out of us.

– Martin Luther

Revival and reformation broke out in Europe and eventually spread to the New World. America became the main beacon of light and truth to the entire world.

Over the last 100 years the world has seen unprecedented revival. Despite the depravity of Europe and America the rest of the world is glowing with the Spirit of God like never before. There are more followers of Jesus alive today than ever before in world history. This is all because of what God did through our Pilgrim fathers. Because of their sacrifices, hundreds of millions of people around the world have received their own personal Bible. It's the word of God that changes lives! Cherish your Bible! It is the living word of God! Millions of people would have risked their lives for that book throughout history. Even today it is an absolute luxury to own one in many parts of the world. Do not take it for granted! It is your main source of intimacy with the living Word himself. We must know the Word personally!

We must shed ourselves of the Romanized ways of Christianity. There is no perfect church and there has never been a perfect Christian. But there is a perfect *Way*! His name is Jesus and we must return to him.

Walls Fall Supernaturally

In the book of Joshua, we read of how God gave the city of Jericho over to the Israelites but required them to first obey a bunch of strange commands. They had to march around the city for days and blow a certain horn made out of a certain material, and there could only be a certain number of men in a certain pattern. We know the wall eventually crumbled at the final trumpet blast because Joshua and his men fulfilled all the Lord's commands, but the series of events can seem rather strange from an outside perspective. It all makes sense, though, once you understand God's point for all the odd instructions.

God doesn't ever send his people into a land just to occupy space; he sends them to take possession of it for his glory. Just prior to the conquest of Jericho, in Joshua chapter 5, Joshua came face-to-face with God. (I believe this was pre-incarnate Jesus.) He refers to himself in the text as the Commander of the Lord's Army. Joshua took off his sandals and worshipped him. The Lord then told Joshua that he was going to give the city of Jericho over to him. We then can wonder, why did Joshua have to do seven days of marching and trumpet blasting? Why didn't the Lord just give the city over to him right there and then? He already said he was going to.

This is where the Lord is making a huge point for all of mankind. *Physical obedience to God releases His supernatural power and will in your life.* The city was already Joshua's when God declared it his. But the Lord wants his children to learn obedience and submission.

We see the same point demonstrated with Moses in Exodus chapter seventeen. Moses was about to enter into battle. God told him if he kept his hands raised, he'd win. And indeed, whenever Moses held up his hands, Israel prevailed, and whenever he lowered his hands, Amalek prevailed. Moses got so tired he had to have Aaron and Hur hold his hands up all through the battle so they would be victorious. (Find friends who will have your back like Aaron and Hur.) Obedience is important to the Lord. He is our Father, after all. Being obedient is not religious; it's being in love with your Father and wanting to please him.

The Goliath sized obstacles do not come down by earthly wisdom. The wall doesn't fall by human understanding. The United States won't be healed by persuasive speech or great political leading. We need to have a face-to-face meeting with the Commander of the Lord's army. Sandals off, face down worshiping him. If the remnant can get to that location, the Lord's feet, in humility, the Lord will then give us his game plan. His game plan might not make sense to our carnal minds. But his ways, his war plans, never fail.

"For my thoughts are not your thoughts, neither are your ways my ways, declares the Lord. For as the heavens are higher than the earth, so are my ways higher than your ways and my thoughts than your thoughts." Isaiah 55:8–9

The *Spirit* of America

We only have true fellowship with God through His Spirit. Before Jesus ascended into heaven he said, "Nevertheless, I tell you the truth: it is to your advantage that I go away, for if I do not go away, the Helper will not come to you. But if I go, I will send him to you" (John 16:7). Jesus is talking about the Holy Spirit, who was sent down from heaven to make his home inside of believers. Think about that for a minute. The Spirit of God has come to make his dwelling place inside of you. The God of the universe dwells inside his body, the church, with Christ being the head. That is why the Holy Spirit always points us back to the one who sent him, Jesus:

"If the Spirit of him who raised Jesus from the dead dwells in you, he who raised Christ Jesus from the dead will also give life to your mortal bodies through his Spirit who dwells in you." Romans 8:11

Earlier this year I met with an elder of Times Square Church in New York. He told me about the church's earlier days with his friend, and pastor, David Wilkerson. Something he told me that David said to him will stick with me forever. Pastor Wilkerson told his church elder and friend, *"If this church ever stops being led by the Holy Spirit you better shut it down, close the door, and lock it!"* The importance of this statement cannot be overlooked. Many church leaders would consider this statement extreme or excessive because they're missing a key fact. The Holy Spirit is God! And without God, you can do nothing! The Christian has relied on his own giftings and wisdom for far too long in America. That is the reason for our nation's spiritual recession. It's time we start relying on Gods Spirit to guide us into revival once again.

It is the Spirit of God that birthed the *Spirit of America*. The Spirit of America is written in our forefather's covenantal prayer, declaring to the whole world that it was "for the glory of God, and advancement of the Christian faith"[87] that our forefathers came here.

I was discussing Eastern world Christianity with Dr.

---

[87] Mayflower Compact 1620

Elijah Kim. If you're not familiar with Dr. Kim, this man has studied over 1000 different Christian revivals in over 170 different countries around the world. There is a heavy anointing on his life. He informed me that the majority of Christianity in the Eastern world where revival is burning is of a "Pentecostal formality." Dr. Kim also told me that he believes the *third great awakening* that Christians have been praying for is going to blossom from New England and more specifically Boston, MA. This resonates with my spirit; I believe New England is certainly ripe for harvest. For many years the typical Christianity in New England has been far from the "Pentecostal way". There is no perfect denomination but perhaps it's the lack of the Holy Spirit in New England that has caused such a spiritual recession. I've heard it said, if we aren't teaching about the Holy Spirit, then Satan is. The pride of man wants to put the Holy Spirit in a box and label what he's capable of. The pride of man will only hinder the Spirit of God.

  The Holy Spirit is not an *it*, he is a person with feelings. You can invite him into a room, and you can push him away. It blows me away when I go to "Christian" weddings and there's an open bar with hard liquor and they're playing profane music. You're inviting spirits to your wedding but not the Holy Spirit.

  When you align your life with the conviction of the Holy Spirit amazing things happen. Miracles even. This is because you give him more territory in your life to move. We often hear of all the miracles happening overseas, and it's true. I was in Africa and I saw a woman go from her deathbed with AIDS to happy and healthy with tested cured blood. But I've seen even greater things happen here in the United States. The same Holy Spirit that raised Jesus from the grave lives in his children and he's not bound to any continent. God moves when you call upon his name in faith! When we truly know and believe the word, our faith allows us to take part in God's work by his Spirit within us.

I've seen cancer healed instantly by prayer, but if I'm being honest, I don't see the results I want all of the time. I want that "stand up and walk" anointing the first apostles had. This doesn't discourage my faith when things don't go my way. It doesn't keep me from praying for anyone with a need because I'm not the one doing the miracle in the first place.

Miracles are an expression of God's love to reveal his glory and draw people to repentance. God knows the individual's heart you are praying for. We do not. Jesus healed ten lepers and only one came back to throw themselves at the feet of Jesus. We have to learn to trust God and just do what the Spirit leads us to do. Sometimes that's laying hands on the sick. Don't hold back the Spirit of God inside of you from other people who need him! Be bold, strong and courageous in Christ!

"Have I not commanded you? Be strong and courageous. Do not be frightened, and do not be dismayed, for the LORD your God is with you wherever you go."

Joshua 1:9

Some people who believe in God have never received the Holy Spirit because they were taught about a false one or they weren't taught about him at all, just like in Acts chapter nineteen when a group of people only received the baptism of John and not the baptism of Jesus. John said himself:

"I baptize you with water for repentance, but he who is coming after me is mightier than I, whose sandals I am not worthy to carry. He will baptize you with the Holy Spirit and fire." Matthew 3:11

Yes, John said *fire*. Don't be afraid of the *fire*. Our God is a consuming *fire*, inside his eyes there is *fire*! The Holy Spirit descended upon the apostles like tongues of *fire*! The Lord descended upon Sinai in a cloud of smoke and *fire*! The burning bush that the Lord sat in was on *fire*! Sanctification is a refining *fire*! The temple sacrifice was consumed by a column of *fire*! Jesus is coming back in the sky with angels and *FIRE*! We all need the *fire* of God in and on our lives to live boldly and courageously for him! Ask God now if you lack his Spirit and *fire*.

"Lord baptize me in the Holy Spirit and *fire*!"

Jezebel

In the books of 1 and 2 Kings, we read about a woman named Jezebel. Jezebel was the wife of King Ahab who seduced him and the nation of Israel into worshiping the sexual gods of Baal and abandoning their worship of Yahweh. Jezebel had a lust for power and control. She was perverted in heart and her mind was overcome by sensuality. In Revelation chapter two, Jesus addresses the same deviational spirit of Jezebel in the church today;

"But I have this against you, that you tolerate that woman Jezebel, who calls herself a prophetess and is teaching and seducing my servants to practice sexual immorality and to eat food sacrificed to idols. I gave her time to repent, but she refuses to repent of her sexual immorality. Behold, I will throw her onto a sickbed, and those who commit adultery with her I will throw into great tribulation, unless they repent of her works, and I will strike her children dead. And all the churches will know that I am he who searches mind and heart, and I will give to each of you according to your works."

Revelation 2:20–23

I'm afraid the American Christian church has become married to the world through compromise. We even look to the world for fashion advice. We desperately need godly women to set the example of modesty for the next generation of women. The next generation needs role models who look less like Hollywood and more like Ruth and Hannah. "Charm is deceitful, and beauty is vain, but a woman who fears the Lord is to be praised" (Proverbs 31:30). Jezebel wants you to amplify your appearance and sex appeal to gain power and control. One person under her spirit can lead an entire congregation astray. The remnant cannot tolerate the spirit of Jezebel. She is a persuasive, perverted pawn of Satan who can manifest her power in any "saint" who opens him or herself up to her. The Christian church in America is in bondage to sexual sin and it's hindering a true move of the Holy Spirit! There have been numerous studies that prove this true. Unfortunately, the numbers are staggering. Even in Christian ministry schools, **one in three** people are addicted to pornography! We have to make the effort to flee, just like Joseph ran from Potiphar's wife who was trying to seduce him. Potiphar's wife was the original desperate housewife looking to drag someone onto her sickbed. Joseph knew better, and we must as well! Run for dear life!

The spirit of Jezebel does not just rest in the realm of sexuality. In fact, sexuality is just one area that she operates in to gain power. Whoever is influenced by her (male or female) is hungry for power and will often acquire leadership positions. Many pastors in America are influenced by Jezebel. They're very similar and often conjoined to the domineering spirit of Saul. Be aware of such leaders. Their speech is drenched in flattery and they only look to use you for what they can get out of you. They will prostitute your giftings and pimp you out to further their movement. They will latch on to those with higher platforms only seeking to exalt themselves and their ministry. Do not be deceived or overcome by this spirit.

I pray that the Holy Spirit will break the chains of Jezebel in your life and in your church. She wants to bring destruction upon Gods people by killing, manipulating and dividing them. She killed many prophets in the Old Testament, and she wants to silence their voice again today. Cast the spirit of Jezebel out the window and let the dogs eat her flesh (2 Kings 9:33). The remnant will not partake in her sorcery!

There cannot be true peace so long as we permit the infidelities and charms of some Jezebel of the soul-life to attract and affect us....Whatever its charms, it must be flung out the window before we can be at peace.

—*F. B Meyer*[88]

---

[88] *Our Daily Homily F. B Meyer*

CHAPTER SIX

Ichabod

What's supposed to separate the church from the world is God himself. I'm talking about the manifest presence of the living God. You can go to many churches across the United States and find that the glory, presence, power, and authority of God is nowhere to be found.

In the book of 1 Samuel, the people of Israel had forgotten the Most High God who delivered them from Egypt. The Lord explained to them plainly how to live according to his word, but the nation of Israel neglected his word and worshiped the false gods of Baal instead. Baal worship included sexual immorality and baby sacrifices in exchange for *prosperity*. Today, Planned Parenthood offers you the same thing after your abortion. The god of Baal (Satan) simply developed another mask. The arch of the temple of Baal was erected in New York City and Washington DC in the name of "history." In ancient times people would walk through this arch to sacrifice their newborn babies. I hope you can see the spiritual significance in this. This physical event in America just signifies the spiritual condition of our fallen nation. There has been a constant flow of blood sacrifice offered to Satan since 1970.

Like America, Israel's continued disobedience was a way of divinely permitting their foes to bring major destruction upon them. Their only hope of winning the battle was turning their hearts back to God. But they didn't do that! They did what was easy, what was in the hands of man to do in their own strength:

And when the people came to the camp, the elders of Israel said, "Why has the LORD defeated us today before the Philistines? Let us bring the ark of the covenant of the LORD here from Shiloh, that it may come among us and save us from the power of our enemies." 1 Samuel 4:3

The Israelites brought forth the Ark of the Covenant, something built by man, thinking certainly this would work, certainly this would earn them the victory. This is an example of external religion and man's agenda to bring revival. Look at the result it produced:

So, the Philistines fought, and Israel was defeated, and they fled, every man to his home. And there was a very great slaughter, for thirty thousand-foot soldiers of Israel fell. And the ark of God was captured, and the two sons of Eli, Hophni and Phinehas, died.[89]

Man was focused on outward, external religion. God was focused on the *hearts* of his people. This kind of thinking led to the slaughter of 30,000 men. God says in his word that he will show strong support to those whose hearts are fully dedicated to him. Israel found out the hard way that you can't manufacture spiritual victories in the flesh. We can play church all we want, but God sees what's really going on inside our souls.

Led by a worldly priesthood, a people whose hearts were far from God put their faith in something made by human hands. They didn't think to look internally but instead looked externally for victory. We see the same in the American church today. We plan out victory and revival by pushing forth our external agenda. Our thought is if we have the right building, follow the right program, have enough money, have the best music, have attracting apparel, have the best preachers, throw the biggest and flashiest conferences, fill all the seats, *then* God will surely give us victory. We could not be more wrong in our thinking! Numbers are not a sign of true fruit! Man is a slave to looking at the outward appearance of the situation. God is always looking inward at the heart of the matter and

---

[89] 1 Samuel 4:10

the heart of the individual in the seat. Man's agenda is how you birth Ichabod:

And she named the child Ichabod, saying, "The glory has departed from Israel!" because the ark of God had been captured and because of her father-in-law and her husband. And she said, "The glory has departed from Israel, for the ark of God has been captured."[90]

It didn't work for Israel, and it won't work for us today. You cannot plan revival. The glory of God, the outpouring of the Holy Spirit, only comes through a true heart cry of repentance. Forget everything else! If the church isn't humble and lowly before the Lord and each other, the glory of God will not be present or bring the victory!

"For the eyes of the Lord run to and fro throughout the whole earth, to give strong support to those whose heart is blameless toward him."

2 Chronicles 16:9

The strong support of the Lord is what brings the victory!

---

[90] 1 Samuel 4:21-22

That is what we need in America once again! That is what Israel needed! A heart that is fully dedicated and blameless toward the Lord. That is what God is in constant search of all over the earth. May he find that here in America once again. May we get over ourselves and get onto our knees. Sackcloth and ashes brought more victory for the men in the Bible than any plan of man's ever did. We have to go low so he can be elevated. God is not a dictator. He gave us dominion over the earth. We have to choose wisely the humble path of subjection to his Spirit and his will in our lives. When God can look at America and see blameless, humble hearts, that is when we will receive his strong support.

Remember the Covenant 1620

A few chapters after Ichabod was birthed in the book of first Samuel, we see that Samuel built a rock monument as a memorial remembering the faithfulness of God. But not before the nation of Israel faced major adversity and went through a true revival of the heart:

Samuel said to all the house of Israel, "If you are returning to the LORD with all your heart, then put away the foreign gods and the Ashtaroth from among you and direct your heart to the LORD and serve him only, and he will deliver you out of the hand of the Philistines."[91]

The nation of Israel was repenting of their sin, turning from their wicked ways, rebuking false gods, and seeking the face of the one true God. As they were giving an offering of repentance to the Lord, the Philistine army tried to attack them. Just then a heavy thunder from the Lord blasted the Philistine army into confusion, and the Israelites defeated them. Samuel then built a stone monument and called it Ebenezer, which means "stone of help." Every time the people of the nation of Israel would pass this monument for hundreds of years, they would remember the revival in the hearts of their forefathers and God's faithfulness to help them through adversity.

America's Ebenezer stone sits on the top of a hill in Plymouth, Massachusetts. It's actually the largest granite monument in the United States of America. At over eighty feet tall, the statue of lady Faith points to heaven with an open Bible clenched in her hand. She is surrounded by four other stone figures sitting on thrones by her feet, each one weighing more than a school bus. The statue commemorates what God did through the sacrifice of our forefathers. It stands as a beacon to our nation, a reminder of what our nation's foundation is. A reminder of the covenant that was made *in the presence of God* 400 years ago on a rocky, wet, cold ship. "Having undertaken, for the Glory of God and advancement of the Christian Faith ... *in the presence of God* and one of another, Covenant and

---

[91] 1 Samuel 7:3

Combine ourselves together into a Civil Body Politic."[92] The Pilgrims understood the importance and necessity of the presence of God and they pledged to live a life that would make a habitation for his presence to rest in.

Engraved in the back of the statue are the words of one of the nation's first governors, William Bradford:

Thus out of small beginnings greater things have been produced by His hand that made all things of nothing and gives being to all things that are; and as one small candle may light a thousand, so the light here kindled hath shone unto many, yea in some sort to our whole nation; let the glorious name of Jehovah have all praise.

This statement engraved into the national forefather's monument simply solidifies the already concrete foundation of the United States. The enemy is trying to blur this from our nation's history books. The majority of all media, education, television, movies, social media, and search engines are controlled by the far left who are very openly against the God of the Bible. This is very serious, and we need to be aware of it. *Google* was just prosecuted in court over controlling and manipulating the information people search for. Think about it. If you search for information about abortion through a website that supports Planned Parenthood, you're going to receive information that glorifies abortion, not exposes it as murder. Big tech is taking over the world slowly but surely. The image of the

---

[92] The Mayflower Compact 1620

beast that people worship in the book of Revelation will likely be technology related.

Even through the madness of our decaying society, our nation's Ebenezer stone stands strong and true overlooking the harbor our forefathers came in through 400 years ago. May it forever remind the world of God's power and provision that established the United States of America to be the lighthouse of the gospel throughout the world. America has sent out more missionaries in the name of Jesus than any other country in the history of the world. That is why God has blessed our nation through adversity. To whom much is given, though, much is required. We must not forget the reason we are blessed in the first place. If we go on abusing the blessing like we have been, if we turn to false gods and vain idols, the hand of God's provision will be removed from our nation. Just like it was from ancient Israel. Look upon the hill in Plymouth and *Remember the Covenant!* Turning our hearts back to the Lord is our nation's only hope.

Cut to the Heart

There are things pertaining to life and the Christian faith we can't explain. A problem arises when mans pride reaches to explain things with certainty that were never actually made certain to us. God keeps us at a humble point of knowledge and understanding. What we need to know has been made crystal clear. We have to realize, for the sake of our oneness that there are some things we don't have a full grasp on. And we probably won't until we meet face to face with God.

I believe we as humans walk in a mysterious space between our free will and God's predestination that only God can see with perfect clarity. Church denominations have been forcing us to pick a side for centuries, but I believe the truth is that we don't exactly know how the relationship between the two works, and I believe there is comfort in that if we just humble ourselves to God's word. I believe life looks something like this:

Free will<   MANKIND   >Predestination

God says that "many are called, but few are chosen" (Matthew 22:14). The Lord wishes that none should perish but that *all* would reach *repentance*. What I believe separates the called from the chosen is our *response* to the *conviction* of Jesus Christ.

The encounter Paul had with Jesus is the only reason more than half of the New Testament exists, and that is only because Paul *repented* after facing the Lords *conviction*.

> "For we know, brothers loved by God, that he has chosen you, because our gospel came to you not only in word, but also in power and in the Holy

Spirit and with full conviction."[93]

The gospel coming in just words is not enough to lead someone to repentance. You can know the Bible in three languages and still not repent of your sin. The gospel has to be received with *full conviction* through the power of the *Holy Spirit.*

The reason the American Christian church has compromised preaching the gospel's full conviction is because we have become people pleasers instead of God pleasers. We've accumulated teachers that teach us what our flesh wants to hear. The modern church attempts to be "nicer" than God and in return manipulates his truth. When we keep our churches full of unrepentant sinners for the sake of numbers, we harm the body of Christ. We say we want the power of the Holy Spirit to move, but yet we hold back from preaching with full conviction.

Reinhard Bonnke said,

"The less Holy Spirit we have, the more cake and coffee we need to keep the church going."[94]

I've also heard it said, "whatever your church catches people on is what they have to keep feeding them." If people come to your church for the wrong reasons, you'll

---

[93] 1 Thessalonians 1:4-5
[94] Evangelist Reinhard Bonnke - Official Facebook Page Reinhard Bonnke, January 8, 2011

be forced to keep feeding them the wrong things to keep them coming back. If you get people consistently coming to church for something other than Jesus, you need to close the doors!

The Bible says you are not a servant of Christ if you seek the approval of man![95] If we hold back and muffle the word of God so that people don't get offended, we aren't preaching with the power of the Holy Spirit and cannot expect people's lives to actually change.

Spurgeon, Meyer, Tozer, Lewis, Moody, McGee, Seymour, Murray, Finney, Wilkerson, and Graham all taught with the unreserved full conviction of God's word. That is why they and *many* others like them are known as heroes of the faith. They did not hold back God's word to suit man's passions and please man's ears. The power of the Holy Spirit will lead you to the full conviction of the gospel if you let him take you there. If you stop him, you are only quenching his power and inhibiting the fulfilment of God's desire for all of mankind; *Reaching repentance.*

The word of God is extremely sharp. It cuts people to the heart. Jesus often preached incredibly convicting messages, never without love of course. In Matthew chapter twenty-three Jesus very firmly rebukes the Pharisees. He completely exposes their wicked hearts and fake godliness. However, he closes the chapter by pouring his heart out to Jerusalem. "How often would I have gathered your children together as a hen gathers her brood

---

[95] Galatians 1:10

under her wings, and you were not willing!"[96] Jesus just wanted to coddle his people like a mother hen coddles her chicks, however they were simply unwilling to submit like children. The pride of man does not like to be tampered with never mind cut to the core.

When you are cut to the heart by God, you can only respond in one of two ways. Repentance or rebellion. When the Spirit of God cuts you to the heart you either become enraged or submissive. There are two accounts in the book of Acts where two different groups of people are quoted as being *cut to the heart* by the apostles preaching. Three thousand repented at the preaching of Peter and the Jewish authorities killed Stephen. Both groups were quoted as being cut to the heart. If you preach with full conviction long enough you will eventually witness the heart response of both audiences.

Paul encountered the full conviction of Jesus on the road to Damascus, and he was blinded for three days. After three years of secret-place sanctification he went out and changed the world. In today's compromised Christian culture, we might assume that blinding Paul was cruel, but it was actually the kindest thing Jesus could have done. God's kindness is meant to bring us to a place of humility, not arrogance:

"Or do you presume on the riches of his kindness and forbearance and patience, not knowing that God's kindness is meant to lead you to repentance?" Romans 2:4

---

[96] Matthew 23:37

God was extremely patient with Paul watching him kill Christians. Paul had no chance of changing his ways until he was met with the full conviction of the Lord.

Preach the full conviction of God's word! Some people will reject you, and the Bible says some will even hate you! The Lord reminds us often, we aren't alive to please man:

> "For am I now seeking the approval of man, or of God? Or am I trying to please man? If I were still trying to please man, I would not be a servant of Christ."[97]

Revival will only come when the full conviction of God's word is preached through the power of the Holy Spirit. We are all called to do the work of an evangelist which is sharing the gospel to people. If we are to preach, we should preach sermons that God would have us preach. Sermons that God gives us in the secret place. Sermons that implore the hearer to repent unto the Lord and live through the power of the Holy Spirit. A heart posture of repentance is not condemning, its humbling. We must never think that we have arrived at some sort of Christian prestige that rests

---

[97] Galatians 1:10

beyond repentance, no matter how long we've been walking with the Lord.

Repentance is a lifestyle of consistently turning to Jesus, not just saying sorry for bad things you did.

Charles Spurgeon understood the vital importance and opportunity of living a lifestyle of repentance, and I think he put it beautifully when he said:

> *It seems to me that every morning when a man wakes up still impenitent, and finds himself out of hell, the sunlight seems to say, "I shine on thee yet another day, as that in this day thou mayest repent." When your bed receives you at night, I think it seems to say, "I will give you another night's rest, that you may live to turn from your sins and trust in Jesus." Every mouthful of bread that comes to the table says, "I have to support your body that still you may have space for repentance." Every time you open the Bible the pages say, "We speak with you that you may repent." Every time you hear a sermon, if it be such a sermon as God would have us preach, it pleads with you to turn unto the Lord and live.*

Lewd Grace

"For certain people have crept in unnoticed who long ago were designated for this condemnation, ungodly people, who pervert the grace of our God into sensuality and deny our only Master and Lord, Jesus Christ."[98]

The perverted grace that Jude is talking about is the same grace that we see so prevalently in America today. This grace simply allows you to continue to live in sin and yet remain in the body of Christ. People under this perverted grace actually go a step further and shamelessly boast in their sin. The word *sensuality* in Jude 1:4 is actually more closely translated in Greek to the word *lewdness*. The ancient Greek word for lewdness would often be used for sin that is sexually boisterous and offensive. This "sexy grace" is a really good sell into todays oversexualized culture. Under this grace you can have your free ticket to heaven and take your favorite sins along for the ride. Lewd grace keeps the church attendance numbers up and it keeps the tithes and offerings flowing in. This grace leads people in a "sinners' prayer" that doesn't include repentance. You just have to accept this grace; no change is necessary. This grace accepts you the way you are. No change required. You are special and unique under this grace. This grace is

---

[98] Jude 1:4

gnostic in nature and narcissistic at heart.

By condoning this perverted grace, we are actually denying our Master and Lord, Jesus Christ. There are two ways to deny the Lord Jesus. You can outright deny him vocally. Or you can deny him by the way you live your life. (Even if you say you accept him.)

This prevalent "lewd grace" is not actually grace at all. For it leads to hell and it keeps you enslaved in sin.

You might ask, what does God's grace do for me then?

"For the grace of God has appeared, bringing salvation for all people, training us to renounce ungodliness and worldly passions, and to live self-controlled, upright, and godly lives in the present age"[99]

The amazing grace of our Lord and savior Jesus Christ actually trains and empowers us to renounce ungodliness and worldly passions. God's grace will even train us to live self-controlled, upright and godly lives. The idea of being in Christ is to actually become more like Christ every day as we grow closer to him. We can only do this through his

---

[99] Titus 2:11-12

grace!

We all have a long road ahead of us, but if we learn to walk in his grace, we can actually start to resemble Jesus. We might not ever stop sinning in this life but by his grace we can be set free from the bondage of sin! It's only through his grace that we can actually change the world around us.

Allow his grace to have its way with you. His true grace will cost you everything. But what you gain in his grace surpasses all the pleasures of Babylon. You gain him. You gain his blood. You gain an abode in his bosom.

If you feel weak and powerless in your attempt to walk in his grace, perfect!

"My grace is sufficient for you, for my power is made perfect in weakness.[100]"

"Therefore, I will boast all the more gladly of my weaknesses, so that the power of Christ may rest upon me. For the sake of Christ, then, I am content with weaknesses, insults, hardships, persecutions, and calamities. For when I am weak, then I am strong."[101]

---

[100] 2 Corinthians 12:9
[101] 2 Corinthians 12:9-10

Vision

There was a construction worker who got to the job site three days early to help his boss with a new project. In just three days the faithful employee built an amazing cobble stone driveway, an Olympic size swimming pool and a grass tennis court. When his boss showed up the next day, he marveled at what he saw. His employee had a big smile on his face waiting to be praised for his amazing work. Then his boss handed him the blueprints for a parking garage.

Having vision is great because where there is no vision the people perish.[102] However, the first question we have to ask ourselves when receiving a vision is, who is the vision coming from? Me or God? Many ambitious men and women come up with extraordinary visions to do good, "Christian" things. Psalm 127:1 tells us, "Unless the LORD builds the house, those who build it labor in vain. Unless the LORD watches over the city, the watchman stays awake in vain." How many ministries, events, conferences and buildings are just a product of man's imagination? When a visionary is prideful you can be assured his vision came from his own imagination and not from God. God warns us about becoming vain in our imaginations (Romans 1:21). He tells us to take every thought captive before Christ and

---

[102] Proverbs 29:18

to cast down imaginations and everything that exalts itself against the knowledge of God (2 Corinthians 10:5).

Romans 1:22–23 says, "Claiming to be wise, they became fools, and exchanged the glory of the immortal God for images resembling mortal man and birds and animals and creeping things."

It was only by man's "vision" that many heretic versions of Christianity were developed. The vain imagination of Charles Russel (the father of the Jehovah's Witnesses) ignited what he believed was the hidden "true" interpretation of the Bible that only he knew. Many men press on through adversity until their vision comes to life and then they label their willpower "faith." Assuredly, faith is not the driving force in these scenarios but the pride of life. It's amazing what pastors will put their flocks through just to see their big dream project come to life. David Wilkerson once wrote,

"All those hours spent poring over plans, spent on site, spent raising money, spent running about—should have been spent in prayer and the study of Gods Word. Men of God are supposed to give themselves to prayer and the Word, and anything that hinders that commitment is robbery. Does God get glory when a shepherd has to fleece the sheep to build his dream project, then keep fleecing them to keep it afloat?"[103]

We must never let ourselves get to this point where

---

[103] David Wilkerson: *Set the Trumpet to thy Mouth,* World Challenge Inc.; First Edition (1985)

we give under compulsion. Where God guides, he provides. Always. God wants us to submit all of ourselves to him including our bank account. The Holy Spirit will instruct you what to give, when to give it and where to give to. "The point is this: whoever sows sparingly will also reap sparingly, and whoever sows bountifully will also reap bountifully. Each one must give as he has decided in his heart, not reluctantly or under compulsion, for God loves a cheerful giver" (2 Corinthians 9:6-7)

We only see God marvel at something twice in the Scriptures. Both times he marvels at faith, once for the shear lack of faith of those in the presence of God and then another time for the greatest faith in Israel. In Matthew chapter eight, a centurion came to Jesus and asked him to heal his servant. Jesus offered to come and heal the man, but the humility of the centurion unlocked even greater faith. He told Jesus, "I'm not worthy for you to come under my roof, but just say the word and my servant will be healed." At this Jesus marveled. I don't know about you, but I want to make Jesus marvel. What we know from Scripture is we're never going to make God impressed with us apart from a leap of humble faith in him. This faith is a gift that is only available through great humility and a greater understanding of who it is that gives us faith.

Habitation

For hundreds of years the Temple of God was a place of habitation for the Lord. *The presence of God,* meaning God himself, dwelt amongst the people in a temple made by human hands. When Christ tore the temple veil in two on the cross, the presence of the Lord was no longer bound by four walls.

A few weeks later the Spirit of God came down from heaven as a rushing wind and found his resting place in temples that were not made with hands. Gods people are now the temple of the living God on earth. We talked about this concept earlier, but I want to expound on this because I believe it will change our lives forever.

Is your life a resting place for the Lord? Does God feel comfortable dwelling in his temple, that is you? Every living thing was designed to find comfort in a specific habitation. Palm trees would never last in New England unless you built a greenhouse. Polar bears would never survive in Florida unless you built a refrigerated zoo. Habitats are either extremely welcoming or extremely rejecting of all that is living. The God of the universe designed life this way and he himself has a specific habitat that makes him comfortable. If the God of the universe has an ideal habitat that makes him comfortable to dwell in, shouldn't it be our goal to build this habitation individually and collectively? When God finds rest in your life and in your meetings, everything changes.

If you're familiar with the revivals of 312 Azusa street in the early 1900's, you'll know they were some of the greatest in American history. Reason being is that 312 Azusa street was a comfortable habitation for the manifest presence of the Lord. There are eyewitness accounts from that old shabby building where heavenly vapor would appear in the air so thick you could cut it with a knife. The fire department would even show up to some meetings because people saw flames shooting from the roof into the sky.

When the heart posture of a room meets the heart posture of heaven amazing things happen. These meetings were multicultural and multi-denominational. The only rule to these meetings was that you'd come in reverence, humility and unity. God wishes that his people would be one as Jesus and the Father are one. That level of unity can only come by dying to self and all of our hidden pride. What keeps meetings like this from happening today are the ulterior motives of the heart. To have a meeting like those on Azusa street you need clean hands and pure hearts. God sees straight through our motives, even if our actions look good on the outside.

True hunger for Jesus changes the atmosphere.

There were two sisters that hosted the presence of Jesus. One was successful and the other was not. Their names are Mary and Martha. Martha thought she had to *do* enough to make Jesus want to stay. The other sister Mary just sat at his feet *beholding* him. Mary was the one who made a comfortable habitation for Jesus, not Martha. In our personal lives and in ministry we can become like Martha very easily, always running around doing "God's work". When all the while God just wants us to sit and behold the Lamb. Mary's way of life has become so contrary to the American Church agenda.

There's so much effort to make God pleased; however, if we truly want to please the Lord, we must make him a comfortable place of habitation. Building a habitation for the Lord starts with our individual lives. "Be holy, for I am holy."[104] God is not looking for lip service, he wants pure heart devotion to him in all areas of our lives. When your life is a resting place for the Lord there is no room for sin because Jesus fills all things! Jesus wants to make you a vessel for honorable use that overflows with new wine and pure oil! There's no room in you for anything else when God inhabits your life! Collectively as the church, God finds rest when we behold him together like Mary. God makes habitation in the praises of his people; he is enthroned in this place![105]

God knows it takes more effort and humility for us to do less sometimes. More can be accomplished by being still and listening than striving intensely after the wind. Such peace came over me the day I finally understood that

---

[104] 1 Peter 1:16
[105] Psalms 22:3

I can't save anyone in my own strength. God calls us to be his hands and his feet. He allows us to take part in his work, but Jesus is the head! It's his job to do the thinking. It's only in the waiting we can hear what the head is actually telling us to do. If we never hear from God, we only do things that we come up with ourselves. It's amazing what man can do without Gods instruction. Silence is not empty space that we have to fill with noise and words. Waiting is not spiritual laziness. It's humility, dependence and discipline.

Thus says the Lord: "Heaven is my throne, and the earth is my footstool; what is the house that you would build for me, and what is the place of my rest? All these things my hand has made, and so all these things came to be, declares the LORD. But this is the one to whom I will look: he who is humble and contrite in spirit and trembles at my word." [106]

There is not a more unpopular word to a Millennial or "Gen Z'r" than *wait*. There has never been a faster paced society than the one we see today. Everything in America is instant—the food, the money, the drugs. Anything that could be considered gratifying to the flesh is instant.

People have been trained by the world to hate waiting for anything. This learned way of life has kept people away from a God who lives in the waiting. God

---

[106] Isaiah 66:1-2

wants to meet with you today in the waiting, the stillness, the quietness of your soul.

"Wait for the Lord; be strong, and let your heart take courage; wait for the Lord!" [107]

"Wait for the Lord and keep his way, and he will exalt you to inherit the land; you will look on when the wicked are cut off." [108]

---

[107] Psalms 27:14
[108] Psalms 37:34

CHAPTER SEVEN

Follow the Rainbow

Homosexuality is a sin, which means it is wrong in the eyes of God to have lustful thoughts or act sexually with someone of the same sex. However, it is not a sin to deeply love the same sex. The apostle John used to intimately rest his head on the chest of Jesus. It is absolutely crucial to understand that *lust* is not *love*. Any lustful thought or action (homosexual or not) is a sin. There are far more people living in heterosexual sexual sin than homosexual sin. Anything that goes against Gods intent for sex is sin. God designed sex for intimacy between one man and one woman. This deep spiritual bond is the way God designed us to take part in creating new life. Sex is a beautiful thing that has been polluted by sin.

I believe the topic of homosexuality has been so mistreated over the years that it now carries a massive false stigma with it. No one is born gay, but no one is born without sin either. A large portion of the LGBT community is actually taking this stance now. LGBT activists are actually pushing for the LGBT to abandon the "born this way" standpoint, because modern science is proving that it simply isn't true and the "born this way" standpoint is making the LGBT look bad.

 Sexuality is a fluid thing that can be perverted into many areas of attraction at any given time in one's life. Thousands of men go into jail straight and come out gay because of the immense perversion that takes place inside some jails. Sexual perversion is powerfully wicked. That is why God also instructs us in his word to not have sex with animals. Sexual perversion is simply any sexual desire that strays away from Gods intended plan and purpose for sexuality.

 There are millions of pedophiles in the world. Let that sink in for a second. Millions of people sexually desire children. It's sickening, I know. Roughly 100,000 children are molested every year in America alone, with millions worldwide. "Sexual abuse (from groping to rape), according to some UNICEF estimates from 2014, affected over **120 million children**..."[109]

Perversion is at the heart of sin and sin is at the heart of man. "The heart is deceitful above all things, and

---

109 https://www.pbc2019.org/protection-of-minors/child-abuse-on-the-global-level

desperately wicked: who can know it?"[110]

Homosexuality is simply perversion of sexuality. Just like pedophilia. Some people are simply born into a progression of circumstances that projects them into living a homosexual lifestyle. I truly believe under specific circumstances *ANYONES* mind can be manipulated into having same-sex attraction. The human mind is very easily manipulated!

Growing up, our minds are like a piece of clay that are formed by hand. How do you think certain Muslim groups get eleven-year-old children to shoot people with machine guns with a smile on their face? It's simply manipulation and indoctrination. That is why Adolf Hitler developed "Hitler's Youth," a program to manipulate the minds of children across Germany. Hitler said, "He alone, who owns the youth, gains the future." Hitler was a mere pawn in the hands of our true enemy, Satan. The younger the child's mind, the more easily it is manipulated. This is basic psychology.

Homosexuality has been around a long time. In ancient Rome, I guess you could say it was mostly "bi-sexuality." Men would have sexual intercourse with anyone they could, even children. It was common practice for men in ancient Rome to raise a young man in apprenticeship while grooming them sexually and raping them for years. This demonic practice has continued to linger in the Roman

---

[110] Jeremiah 17:9

lineage of the Catholic Church. This depraved mindset has always been around because sin has always been around. That is why God gave us his word to live by, for our own benefit.

The homosexual community needs to encounter the love of God. We must love the person living in homosexuality. Jesus died for all of mankind's sin, including homosexuality. The person living in homosexuality can lose their same-sex attraction, I'm positive. I know several people personally who have lost their desire for the same sex and now have prosperous God honoring heterosexual marriages. It's the same way that the porn addict loses their desire for porn, through the washing of the mind with the word of God, sanctification, prayer, and fasting. *Jesus sets us free!*

As of right now one of the most serious attacks against religious freedom in 400 years is being heavily pushed forward. They are calling this heinous bill the "Equality Act," which is far from bringing equality. The scariest thing about this bill is how few people are even aware of its existence. Dr. James Dobson said, "It imposes a thinly veiled death sentence to the First Amendment of the Constitution and takes away the protections against tyranny handed down to us by our Founding Fathers."[1] If

---

[1] Dr. James Dobson, "Dr. James Dobson Condemns House Democrats for Passing what Should be Called 'The Inequality Act of 2019,'" May 20, 2019, https://www.drjamesdobson.org/about/latest-news/news-media/2019/05/20/dr.-james-dobson-condemns-house-democrats-for-passing-what-should-be-called-'the-inequality-act-of-2019'.

this bill passes, no one will legally be allowed to preach the fullness of God's word. This bill would basically put gender identity and sexual orientation into the same category as race. Under this bill, any verbal opposition to same-sex marriage would be considered hate speech. I hope you see the severity of this spiritual attack and would actively and prayerfully stand against it, for the religious freedom and wellbeing of our nation and the generations to come.

Currently in Massachusetts, it is criminal to openly oppose someone who identifies as transgender. If a 6'4 man with a beard enters the women's gym locker room behind your 16-year-old daughter, you are not allowed to legally confront him if he "identifies" as a woman. This bathroom bill slipped through the cracks because the church at large has been dead asleep.

The rainbow is a symbol that God created to represent a covenant he made with mankind. The rainbow is a beautiful promise of love and grace:

And God said, "This is the sign of the covenant that I make between me and you and every living creature that is with you, for all future generations: I have set my bow in the cloud, and it shall be a sign of the covenant between me and the earth. When I bring clouds over the earth and the bow is seen in the clouds, I will remember my covenant that is between me and you and every living creature of all flesh. And the waters shall never again become a flood to destroy all flesh. When the bow is in the clouds, I will see it and remember the everlasting covenant between God and every living creature of all flesh that is on the earth." God said to Noah, "This is the sign of the covenant that I have established between me and all flesh that is on the earth." Genesis 9:12–17

In heaven, God's throne is encircled by a rainbow. Covenants are extremely important in the eyes of God. Especially his own. The first covenant God created was the covenant of marriage. One man, one woman, for one lifetime. This beautiful relationship between man and woman is a representation of the deep intimacy between Christ Jesus and his bride, the church.

Unfortunately, we have wandered far from God's original intended purpose for life. One of the darkest days in American history was the day that two covenants of God were blasphemed for the world to see. The covenant of the rainbow and the covenant of marriage were projected in color upon the White House in 2015. Man took what was God's and redesigned it to suit his own passions. Since then, the sexual perversion of America has only progressed, to the point now that there are literally "support pedophilia" movements on the rise. There was even a *TEDx* talk that attempted to normalize Pedophilia! People clapped for it!

Once you blur the lines of morality, it's all over. It's like punching a hole in a dam wall. The water slowly corrodes the rest of the dam until the river blows it all apart.

Our fight is not against the person living in homosexuality. We are to love them like Jesus loves us! Our fight is not of flesh and blood. This is a spiritual attack against the body of Christ, and if the church doesn't wake up and join the battle, we will lose. The pressure to conform to the patterns of this world is growing. Big tech is closing in on total control. The internet juggernauts are slowly silencing the voice of the remnant. The persecution of the remnant in America is just beginning. Christians worldwide are going to be imprisoned for standing against this sin.

Follow the rainbow, it is a prophetic message that points to the end of this age.

"But as the days of Noah were, so shall also the coming of the Son of man be."[111]

"The Lord saw that the wickedness of man was great in the earth, and that every intention of the thoughts of his heart was only evil continually."[112]

---

[111] Matthew 24:37
[112] Genesis 6:5

Signs in Sun and Moon

There is a significant and important correlation between Israel and America. Our Judeo-Christian heritage is the fabric with which our government was created. The nation of Israel are God's covenantal people. The United States was established upon the new covenant that grafted Gentiles into Gods family through the blood of Jesus. The United States "covenant form" of government was based off of the Puritans' view of Israel's covenant with God. America began in agreement that our rights, laws, and morals originated with our Creator. This covenant was established 400 years ago in Plymouth, Massachusetts.

I was talking to a pastor from Florida, a very loving, humble man who I recently found out was in the Special Forces for 14 years. He told me a story from back in the early 2000's that stuck with me forever. He was fasting and praying with a group of pastors when the Lord led them to the National Forefathers Monument in Plymouth, MA. As they were in deep communion with the Lord, he looked up and saw an angel standing in front of the National Forefathers Monument. He asked the Lord, "What is this angel doing here?" The Lord told him, "He's watching over the covenant."

John Winthrop was the first governor of the Massachusetts Bay Colony. Over a sixteen-year period he led over 16,000 puritans who were under persecution in

England out of England and into freedom in Massachusetts. This is known as the Great Puritan Migration, which took place roughly ten years after the original landing of the Pilgrims in Plymouth in 1620. John Winthrop said,

"It is of the nature and essence of every society to be knit together by some covenant, either expressed or implied...We are a Company, professing ourselves fellow members of Christ, we ought to account ourselves knit together by this bond of love...It is by a mutual consent through a special overruling Providence...to seek out a place of Cohabitation...under a due form of Government both civil and ecclesiastical....Thus stands the cause between God and us: we are entered into covenant with Him for this work."[113]

The real essence of what God was doing through the entire pilgrimage to the New World was that he was preserving a remnant of his people out of Europe that would light the world with the gospel. The pilgrims were the persecuted church, just like Noah and his family who were openly mocked for their faith. Just like God has done time and time again with his people Israel, God always preserves a remnant, and that is why we stand here free today in America. We are the fruit of the remnant of 1620,

---

[113] https://myemail.constantcontact.com/William-Brewster---the-Pilgrim-Covenant.html?soid=1108762609255&aid=3HOTbnVwFtk

preserved by God. I truly believe over the course of 400 years we've come so far off from what God started here that he is now preserving a remnant once again to reestablish the covenant he decreed over our founding fathers and our nation.

There is something biblically significant about the time frame of 400 years and the number 400 itself. God was preparing his nation Israel for roughly 400 years while they were in slavery in Egypt. The ministry of the prophets was roughly 400 years. The time span of the seven judges of Israel was roughly 400 years. The divided kingdom lasted roughly 400 years. There were 400 years from Malachi to the New Testament. Esau pursued Jacob with 400 men. In the book of Judges, 400 virgins married 400 men of the tribe of Benjamin. Abraham purchased his wife's burial site for 400 shekels. There were 400 pomegranates that hung in the first temple. There were 400 sheep sacrificed in the second temple. I'm sure I'm missing some, but I think the point is clear. There is simply something significant to God about the number 400.

In 2020, the United States will celebrate the 400th anniversary of our forefathers' arrival in Plymouth, Massachusetts. 2020 will mark the 400th year of the New World's covenantal beginnings. This covenant is protecting America, and I'm convinced that there's an angel protecting the covenant.

God revealed something very significant to me and the trumpet must be sounded on this matter. Something of biblical proportion is happening before our eyes. I believe God is clearly marking the 400th anniversary of America on his celestial calendar. I'm not an expert in astronomy, but the United States of America has only undergone a couple of total solar eclipses that were exclusive to the United States, one of them being the Great American Eclipse of 2017. A total solar eclipse is the rarest event of the sun and the moon.

First, I want to talk about what is known as "the most famous solar eclipse in history." On June 15th, 763BC the Assyrian Empire (modern day Iraq) was shadowed under a total solar eclipse that left its capital city in mid-day darkness for five straight minutes. You can imagine the impact this would have on an ancient civilization. It would be utter chaos. The empires capital city was none other than Nineveh. Nineveh was the most wicked city of its era in the likeness of Sodom and Gomorrah. Nineveh is usually affiliated with the story of the prophet Jonah who God forcefully brought there to preach repentance of sin. Jonah would likely be killed for doing so but somehow Jonah was well received and the city mourned, fasted and repented of their sin. The prophet Jonah came to Nineveh around the same time frame that this total solar eclipse passed over the land, possibly even within days.

In 1979 Assyriologist and archeologist Donald Wiseman, who was also curator at the British Museum, published a lecture in the *Tyndale Bulletin*[114] where he argued that this solar eclipse was the key element that made Jonah so well received in Nineveh. According to Dr. Wiseman there was a series of Assyrian interpretation for this eclipse that would have been, "'the king will be deposed and killed, and a worthless fellow seize the throne'; 'the king will die, rain from heaven will flood the land. There will be famine'; 'a deity will strike the king and fire consume the land'."[115]

Jesus said clearly that some end times signs will take place in the sun and moon. "And there will be signs in sun and moon..." (Luke 21:25). God created these celestial bodies to relay messages. We must pay attention to these signs of the times!

The very first page of the Bible explains that God made two great lights. One to govern the night and the greater light to govern the day. What is often overlooked is that God also instructs us on the first page of the Bible that the sun and moon would be used for signs! "And God said, "Let there be lights in the expanse of the heavens to separate the day from the night. And let them be for *signs* and for seasons, and for days and years."[116]

With that being said, I want to start explaining this

---

[114] https://legacy.tyndalehouse.com/tynbul/Library/TynBull_1979_30_02_Wiseman_JonahsNineveh.pdf
[115] https://legacy.tyndalehouse.com/tynbul/Library/TynBull_1979_30_02_Wiseman_JonahsNineveh.pdf
[116] Genesis 1:14

by looking at the most powerful celestial sign in American history. This is a quote from *USA Today*:

"On Aug. 21, 2017, a total solar eclipse will be visible from coast to coast, according to NASA. It will be the first total eclipse visible only in the USA since the country was founded in 1776."[1]

So, before 2017 the last total solar eclipse over America took place the year the Declaration of Independence was signed. This was certainly a significant event. This got me wondering, what was the significance of the eclipse in 2017? Or was there any significance about it at all?

2017 is the year that president Trump declared that Jerusalem was Israel's capital. That was certainly a biblically significant event. But nothing really clicked until I discovered that there is going to be another total solar eclipse ***seven years*** later on April 8, 2024. I had to ask myself, "How could something so rare happen twice so close in time?" Interestingly enough, the 2024 eclipse will make a giant shadow X as it crosses over our nation paired

---

[1] Doyle Rice, "200 million people are within just one day's drive of the solar eclipse. What you need to know," *USA Today*, June 30, 2017, https://www.usatoday.com/story/tech/science/2017/06/29/americas-total-solar-eclipse-what-you-need-know/439544001/.

with the path of the eclipse of 2017.

    The kicker is the timeframe that falls directly in the middle of that 7-year window is mid-December 2020. This is **EXACTLY** 400 years from when the remnant of 1620 dropped their anchor in Plymouth Bay! I believe that God is marking with a big shadow X the 400th anniversary of our nations true, providential, Christ centered, covenantal beginnings in Plymouth![117]

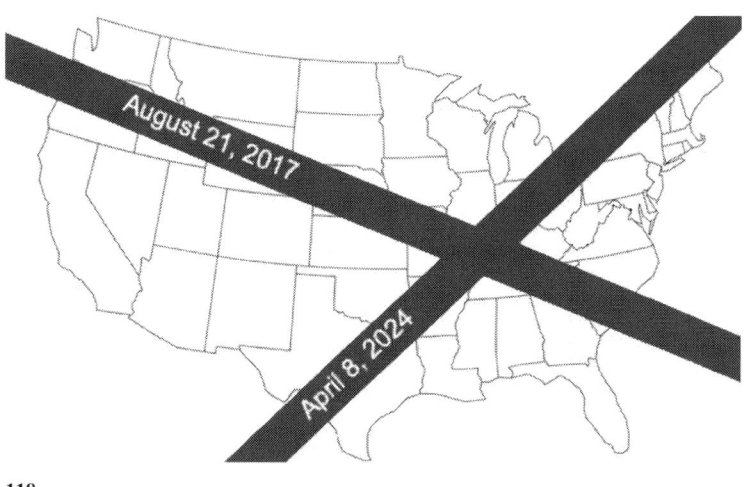

[118]

This is clearly a sign from heaven that marks America. I believe the message is clear and simple. I believe God is

---

[117] In the 2020 State of the Union address, President Donald Trump recognized Plymouth, MA heritage in an unprecedented way.
[118] Authors rendition of the eclipse map is not exact proportions.

sending the USA the same message that he sent to Nineveh. *Repent of your sins and seek my face!*

Seek His Face

In front of me on my desk right now sits a silver coin from the Temple Institute in Israel. It has two faces on the front of it: President Donald Trump and King Cyrus. We know President Trump well, but recall who King Cyrus was:

"In the first year of Cyrus king of Persia, that the word of the LORD by the mouth of Jeremiah might be fulfilled, the LORD stirred up the spirit of Cyrus king of Persia, so that he made a proclamation throughout all his kingdom and also put it in writing:

"Thus says Cyrus king of Persia: The LORD, the God of heaven, has given me all the kingdoms of the earth, and he has charged me to build him a house at Jerusalem, which is in Judah." Ezra 1:1–2

On the back of the coin that sits on my desk there is a detailed image of the future third temple. The Jewish people believe when this temple is built the Messiah will rule them there. What they refuse to see is that they'll be misled by a false messiah first. Then the true Messiah, our

Lord Christ Jesus will come down from heaven with Angels and fire. He will split the mount of Olives in two and speak the antichrist into dust. Every knee will bow, and every tongue WILL confess that Jesus Christ is Lord! To the glory of God, the Father.

The image of the third temple paired with the faces of President Trump and King Cyrus is very significant. Israel is honoring Trump as today's "Cyrus", because on the 70th anniversary of Israel, President Trump declared to the world that Jerusalem was Israel's capital. This declaration, along with the relocation of the US Embassy to Jerusalem, sparked a major shift in end times Bible prophecy.

Now, Israel is encouraging President Trump to go all the way with his declaration and initiate the building of the third temple. I believe this could very well happen if President Trump wins this coming election. Nevertheless, the third temple will be built because God says so in his word, just as he predicted the destruction of the second temple in his word.

The ancient historian Flavius Josephus told us in his writings that the believed temple mount is actually the old Roman fort and that the temple was actually built in the city of David next to the current day dome of the rock. This is a growing belief of many Jews in Israel. I believe Josephus because Jesus said himself, "There will not be left here one stone upon another that will not be thrown down" (Matthew 24:2). The believed western wall is still in place.

That is why I join Josephus and many others that there is no stone left unturned of the old temple. If this becomes common knowledge the temple will be erected in the city of David which is next to the temple mount.

Either way, when the day comes that we see the third temple being built, regardless of its exact location, we must understand the weight of this event. The third temple is one of the single greatest signs of the end of end times. Regardless of your stance on the time frame of the rapture of the church, do not be deceived by a false return of Christ. There will be no mistaking the true return of Christ. The Antichrist will come with false signs and wonders. The remnant that knows Jesus and his word will not be misled by false signs because when you know someone intimately there is no mistaking their identity. I pray that a remnant stronger than any before rises up in these last days, just like after the declaration of King Cyrus:

"But now for a brief moment favor has been shown by the Lord our God, to leave us a remnant and to give us a secure hold within his holy place," Ezra 9:8

For a brief moment favor has been shown to you. The last days remnant will undergo persecution like no Christians have ever faced in American history. We must be built up and ready to face it with boldness, love, joy, and thanksgiving.

God is marking the United States with an X of solar eclipse shadows. I believe this is his way of telling America to repent and seek his face while we still can. Repentance was the cry of John the Baptist before the first coming of the Lord Jesus. How much more will the cry of repentance echo before the second coming of the Lord Jesus!

If you imagine the sun representing God's face and the moon as a covering, I believe it is symbolic of God giving us a grace period to repent as a nation. I believe 2017-2024 is a 7-year window of opportunity.

When we look at the Holy Scriptures, we see nothing but pure, unfathomable power pouring out of the face of God. The face of God pours out his judgement and his blessing. The face of God is the most glorious thing in existence. The Bible tells us that no man can see it and live. The Scriptures are chock full of verses referencing the face of God. There are so many scriptures I left out for the sake of your time, but please, read the following carefully. They convey the point clearly enough.

O LORD God of hosts, restore us;

Cause Your face to shine upon us, and we will be saved. (Psalm 80:19 NASB)

And He will strike the earth with the rod of His mouth,

And with the breath of His lips He will slay the wicked. (Isaiah 11:4 NASB)

His lips are filled with indignation And His tongue is like a consuming fire; (Isaiah 30:27 NASB)

"I will not hide My face from them any longer, for I will have poured out My Spirit on the house of Israel," declares the Lord GOD. (Ezekiel 39:29 NASB)

"I will set My face against you so that you will be struck down before your enemies; and those who hate you will rule over you, and you will flee when no one is pursuing you." (Leviticus 26:17 NASB)

So, we see clearly that either blessing or destruction pours out of the face of God. Yet we also see a third option: God can hide his face from us. When God hides his face from us it can allow free will persecution to come upon us, but it can also save us from the righteous judgment of God.

Our God is a consuming fire. If he were to shine his face upon America right now, I don't think blessing would pour out. I think we would receive the rod of his mouth and the smoke of his nostrils. I believe that God is hiding his face from us because he loves us and it's a form of grace upon our nation. He's protecting America by shielding his face because there is still a remnant that intercedes for America.

When God hides his face from us it doesn't remove his presence. Moses was in the direct presence of God but was only allowed to see his back. He wasn't allowed to see his face. We see in the word that when a people humble themselves and truly seek God's face in repentance, that's when God turns his face and pours out provision and blessing. And on the contrary, I believe that the judgment poured out on Sodom and Gomorrah was simply a result of God turning his face toward the cities. I believe that God just simply looked upon them with his face through the clouds and judgement was poured out on their wickedness. I believe that is why no one was allowed to look back at the cities and live. I believe Lot's wife saw the face of God that day and that is why she turned into a pillar of salt.

God was just by his own measure to preserve a remnant out of Sodom and Gomorrah, and he is just to preserve a remnant in America today. Who will intercede like Abraham? Do not forget what Jesus said about the town that rejects him:

"Truly, I say to you, it will be more bearable on the day of judgment for the land of Sodom and Gomorrah than for that town." Matthew 10:15

I believe God is giving America a seven-year grace period between 2017 and 2024. I believe that what we do in this window will shape the future of our nation and that in 2024 the window will close. I believe our two options are this: repent, seek the face of God and have him turn his face upon us and receive blessing and the outpouring of his Holy Spirit. Or, continue to digress into wickedness and bring further judgment and destruction on our nation.

Lord willing in the fall of 2020 there will be a worldwide prayer meeting from Plymouth, Massachusetts. The "heart cry" of the prayer meeting will be one of repentance for our nation and a request unto the Lord for a third great awakening in America. This needs to remain our heart cry until we see major breakthrough in America.

We don't have to fully understand God, because we never could. What we are called to do is fear him, humble ourselves, turn from our wicked ways, and seek his face and he *will* bring healing to our land. God's promises are concrete. We built our country on his word so we could stand on his promises.

The main call of the remnant is to seek the face of God in all humility. Jesus is the image of the invisible God. We are able to see the face of Jesus and live. That is why, I believe, Jacob wrestled with Jesus and Moses met face-to-face with Jesus. When you seek the face of God, you seek Jesus. Life itself is in the eyes of Jesus. Fire too. The eyes are at the center of the face! Seek Jesus! Seek the face of God!

*"if my people who are called by my name humble themselves, and pray and **seek my face** and turn from their wicked ways, then I will hear from*

*heaven and will
forgive their sin and
heal their land."*
2 Chronicles 7:14

The way to live a righteous, God-honoring, holy, sanctified life in the power of the Holy Spirit is simplified in one passage of scripture. Matthew 14:22–23 is where Jesus walks on water. If you want to walk on water, or in other words do as Jesus did, you must simply maintain eye contact with Jesus. Peter walked on water by faith in the one he was staring at. As long as Peter's eyes stayed locked on Jesus he was living in the supernatural. There's a difference between you and Jesus. But there is no difference between you and Peter. What's more impressive, walking on water or speaking to a mountain and watching it move? The word shows us that both can be done in faith. Faith itself is built in the history of your eye contact with Jesus. When you gaze upon him intently, you see clearly the reality of your existence. As soon as Peter took his eyes off of Jesus, he sank. Everything else in this life that is not the eyes of Jesus is the wind and the waves.

You desire to live a sanctified life. I applaud your obedience! But you will fail if you focus on your sin! The way to stop sinning is to reposition your eyes from your sin to the eyes of Jesus! The way to walk by faith is to reposition your eyes from the mountain in front of you to the eyes of Jesus! The way to live joyfully is to reposition your eyes from your problems to the eyes of Jesus! The way to live in freedom is to reposition your eyes from fear to the eyes of Jesus! This is the secret to living an abundant, powerful, prosperous, and sanctified life. You must stay in a constant, deep gaze into the eyes of Jesus. That's where miracles happen. That's where faith is built. And that's where true life is found. *In the eyes of Jesus. The image, the face of God.*

Let's focus in on *Ezekiel 15:7.*

"And I will set my face against them. Though they escape from the fire, the fire shall yet consume them, and you will know that I am the Lord, when I set my face against them."

The Lord wasn't talking to a foreign, pagan enemy of his people. He was talking to his own people!

"I will set my face against them"

This doesn't mean that the Lord would hide his face or turn his face away in disgust. This literally means that Lord would set his face (his direct presence) in opposition of his own people.

America as a whole is deeply grieving the Lord but

not as much as his own people are grieving him. America is already under judgment. It will worsen as the nation continues to push God out, but the God hating wrath of man that is set against all things holy in America can only affect God so much.

Historically what moves the heart of God to set his face against a people is when it's HIS people that hurt him. What brings the most righteous fury out of the Lord is when his own bride cheats on him with the world! The next chapter (Ezekiel 16) talks about the Lords faithless bride. The chapter starts off by romantically describing the Lords deep intimacy and care for his people, his bride. However, not even halfway through the chapter the Lords bride strips herself of all that God has given her and uses her gifts to whore around with other nations and partake in their idolatry. My friends this is America, and even worse this is the American Christian Church at large. Compromise after compromise the church has conformed to the patterns of this world. God will set his face against us if we continue to break his heart. We need to return to first love intimacy with the Lord. He must take preeminence in ALL areas of our lives. We must seek his face with all that we have.

Americas Final Warning

Americas final warning was prophetically written roughly 400 years ago. John Winthrop was the pioneer of The Great Puritan Migration. John Winthrop was a mighty man of God. As I said before, he led over 16,000 puritan men, women and children to New England over the course of about a decade.

I wrote the majority of this book at lot #1 in America[119], the first house site, which is the first house of prayer in America. This is also the location of the first Thanksgiving that we celebrate today and the same location where the peace treaty with the Native Americans was signed. This is the longest lasting peace treaty in American history. I've seen actual purchase agreements transferring land from Native Americans to Englishmen. The truth is they had great relations for many years and the gospel flourished in a lot of the Native American communities. The entire island of *Noepe* (Martha's Vineyard) became known as *salvation island*! American sign language was even invented to bring the deaf people of the Island the gospel message.

There has always been a pure stream of the power and presence of God flowing through the remnant of Gods true people. Unfortunately, these remnant believers of the early 1600's are overshadowed by the many religious

---

[119] More info visit *theremnant.net*

zealots who followed and brought the corrupt ways of King James to New England with them. They are the ones that lived blasphemous, disgraceful lives that we hear about stampeding over Native American land. Even then, a lot of those stories have been manipulated to fit a false narrative that wishes to remove God from America.

Nevertheless, the seed of the remnant carried on in America and it's the purity of their God-fearing lives and prayers that reaped the blessing on this nation, **not** the crusade like religious zealots that trampled over Native Americans.

John Winthrop left the remnant with one of the most profound statements in US history. I believe this was actually a prophetic message for us now in 2020, whether Winthrop knew it or not. Please take the time to read this final warning message that is more relevant today for the remnant of 2020 than it was for the remnant of 1620:

> *Now the only way to avoid this shipwreck, and to provide for our posterity, is to follow the counsel of Micah, to do justly, to love mercy, to walk humbly with our God. For this end, we must be knit together, in this work, as one man. We must entertain each other in brotherly affection. We must be willing to abridge ourselves of our superfluities, for the supply of others' necessities. We must uphold a familiar commerce together in all meekness, gentleness, patience and liberality. We must delight in each other; make others' conditions*

*our own; rejoice together, mourn together, labor
and suffer together, always having before our eyes
our commission and community in the work, as
members of the same body. So shall we keep the
unity of the spirit in the bond of peace. The Lord
will be our God, and delight to dwell among us, as
His own people, and will command a blessing upon
us in all our ways, so that we shall see much more
of His wisdom, power, goodness and truth, than
formerly we have been acquainted with. We shall
find that the God of Israel is among us, when ten of
us shall be able to resist a thousand of our enemies;
when He shall make us a praise and glory that men
shall say of succeeding plantations, "may the Lord
make it like that of New England." For we must
consider that we shall be as a city upon a hill. The
eyes of all people are upon us. So that if we shall
deal falsely with our God in this work we have
undertaken, and so cause Him to withdraw His
present help from us, we shall be made a story and
a by-word through the world. We shall open the
mouths of enemies to speak evil of the ways of God,
and all professors for God's sake. We shall shame
the faces of many of God's worthy servants, and
cause their prayers to be turned into curses upon us
till we be consumed out of the good land whither we
are going.*

*And to shut this discourse with that exhortation of
Moses, that faithful servant of the Lord, in his last*

farewell to Israel, Deut. 30. "Beloved, there is now set before us life and death, good and evil," in that we are commanded this day to love the Lord our God, and to love one another, to walk in his ways and to keep his Commandments and his ordinance and his laws, and the articles of our Covenant with Him, that we may live and be multiplied, and that the Lord our God may bless us in the land whither we go to possess it. But if our hearts shall turn away, so that we will not obey, but shall be seduced, and worship other Gods, our pleasure and profits, and serve them; it is propounded unto us this day, we shall surely perish out of the good land whither we pass over this vast sea to possess it.

Therefore let us choose life,

that we and our seed may live,

by obeying His voice and cleaving to Him,

for He is our life and our prosperity.[1]

We can't be so ignorant as to believe that the blessing on this nation is irrevocable. God gives and he takes away. Let

---

[1] John Winthrop, "A Model of Christian Charity," *A Library of American Literature: Early Colonial Literature, 1607–1675*, ed. Edmund Clarence Stedman and Ellen Mackay Hutchinson, (New York: 1892), 304–307.

this warning of John Winthrop develop a heart cry in you to repent for your nation. God will not be mocked. If we are seduced to worship false gods, our pleasures, and our profits, we will surely perish out of this great land. The United States is on a treacherous road. The only way to avoid this impending shipwreck is to humble ourselves, repent of our sinful ways and seek the face of God.

If America doesn't answer the remnant call of "IF" (2 Chronicles 7:14) our destiny is answered in the passage that follows. John Winthrop's prophetic message highly reflects the following scripture.

"But if you turn aside and forsake my statutes and my commandments that I have set before you, and go and serve other gods and worship them, then I will pluck you up from my land that I have given you, and this house that I have consecrated for my name, I will cast out of my sight, and I will make it a proverb and a byword among all peoples. And at this house, which was exalted, everyone passing by will be astonished and say, 'Why has the Lord done thus to this land and to this house?' Then they will say, 'Because they abandoned the Lord, the God of their fathers who brought them out of the land of Egypt, and laid hold on other gods and worshiped them and served them. Therefore he has brought all this disaster on them.'"[120]

---

[120] 2 Chronicles 7:19-22

Sound the shofar! It is time for a call to repentance in the land. **Sound it again** to seek the face of God! **Sound it once more**, a call for the remnant to unite! It is time to take back what the enemy has stolen. This is covenant land! We need to restore the covenant! It is truly now or never!

The Great Falling Away

Historically, *The Way* thrives under persecution. At some point soon Christians could be forced into complying with government mandates on gender and sexuality or be legally persecuted. You may think this sounds extreme, but this is already progressing quickly in parts of the country. There is militant push from LGBT activist to legally end any public speech against homosexuality or "gender identity". This movement is funded by some of the wealthiest people in the world.

In this upcoming presidential election one of the top priorities of the current president's opposition is to remove the tax-exempt status of any church that will not conduct homosexual marriages. This is just the start of their bigger plan which is to press legal charges against people who preach against homosexuality. A pastor in Canada was already arrested while lovingly preaching against the sin of homosexuality.

I believe there is a window of opportunity for repentance that we talked about. If we do not revoke abortion and same sex marriage, we will surely perish out of this good land.

The pendulum is coming back quickly, and when it does it will be the end of America as we know it.

America will reap the fruit of its whorish idolatry. We have simply rebelled against God as a nation. While the church slept and continues to sleep the enemy is quickly sowing his own seed of deception and confusion. The children of generation Z are growing up in a completely new America with a completely new version of right and wrong.

You cannot remove the foundation of America, which is the rock Jesus Christ, and expect the nation to stay standing. America has forgotten why it is a blessed nation in the first place. The blessing will be removed if its foundation is removed. If we continue on this path, America will meet the same fate as Sodom and Gomorrah or perhaps Nineveh.

I recently had a vivid vision in the night of the National Forefathers Monument's center figure, lady faith. In the vision, she was holding a dead stone child and she was weeping over him bitterly. I believe this was a prophetic message of our forefathers' faith weeping over an entire generation.

The last days are upon us. The labor pains are

intensifying. Stay awake and do not be seduced to worship false idols. Christ is coming back like a thief in the night and he's coming back to take his bride.

The same word in the Greek, *harpazo*, is used multiple times to explain what the rapture really is. *Harpazo* means "to be snatched up, seized or carried away by force." When Jesus ascended into heaven, he was *harpazo'd*. When Paul was caught up in the third heaven, he was also *harpazo'd*. Philip was *harpazo'd* after baptizing the Ethiopian eunuch. The word *harpazo* is a supernatural (interdimensional) relocating of an individual.

In the case of the rapture, we read,

"Then we who are alive, who are left, will be caught up together [*harpazo'd*] with them in the clouds to meet the Lord in the air, and so we will always be with the Lord."[121]

The remnant that is left will be *harpazo'd* into the clouds with the Lord. This event will take place before the second coming of the Lord. How glorious a day this will be.

...for that Day will not come unless the falling away comes first...[122]

There is going to be a great falling away before the *harpazo* of the remnant, and before the Antichrist claims to be God on earth. I believe we are currently in the beginning stages

---

[121] 1 Thessalonians 4:17
[122] 2 Thessalonians 2:3

of this great falling away here in America. The Methodist church, which is one of the largest denominations of Christianity, just announced that they are dividing over the topic of homosexuality and gender.

By the time generation Z is in their 30's it is estimated that roughly 40 million people in America will depart from the Christian Faith.

The Greek word used for the great falling away is *apostasia*. Which literally means to depart from your stand or depart from your state of being. There is not a clearer departure from one's state of being than this mass wave of gender confusion in America. Men are "transforming" into women. Women are "transforming" into men. Thousands of adults are giving little children hormone injections to "change" their gender.

Gods moral code is being removed from America brick by brick. The foundation of America is corroding into the sea. We are in the dawn of the great apostasia! I hear the voice of the Prophets echoing in the wind,

"Repent, for the kingdom of heaven is at hand."[123]

There is an urgency in these last days! The same urgency of the garden of gethsemane when Jesus told his disciples to stay awake and pray with him! Many will be deceived in

---

[123] Matthew 3:2

these last days. We must stay awake with Christ and pray fervently! *"Watch and pray that you may not enter into temptation. The spirit indeed is willing, but the flesh is weak."*[124] Jesus had to tell his disciples to stay awake three times! The American church has been sleeping and I feel as if Christ is coming back for the third time to say,

"stay awake!"

"Sleep and take your rest later on. See, the hour is at hand..."[125]

Stay awake! Now is the time to labor in prayer!

"And a young man named Eutychus, sitting at the window, sank into a deep sleep as Paul talked still longer. And being overcome by sleep, he fell down from the third story and was taken up dead.[126]"

Brothers and sisters the American Christian church is in a *Eutychus* state of being. We lay three stories down breathless in the dust awaiting a *Paul* generation that knows who they are in Christ Jesus. A generation who moves in the power of the Holy Spirit. A generation who has counted the cost and lives hard-pressed between fruitful labor and death. A generation that will resurrect the church from its lifeless state of being!

---

[124] Matthew 26:41
[125] Matthew 26:45
[126] Acts 20:9

Now is the time to wake up! Now is the time to revive the lifeless church!

"Wake up, and strengthen what remains and is about to die, for I have not found your works complete in the sight of my God." Revelation 2:3

Rise up and take part! Now is the time to plow the fields! Don't look back! The latter rains are coming to America! Take part in the harvest!

The harvest is plentiful, but the remnant is few!

With all love, humility and unity.
Join the harvest.
Join *The Remnant*.

Made in the USA
Columbia, SC
05 June 2020